Praise for African Children's Manifesto:

"For those who refuse to accept what is really one of the main causes why schools around this country are failing students of African ancestry, this book will be dismissed as left-wing dogma. For those who are sincere about creating schools where Black children can thrive, this book will be an invaluable guide. Hard-hitting, yet easy to understand, *African Children's Manifesto* will be simultaneously eye-opening and liberating for parents whose children have not done well in America's 'traditional' school settings."

Debra Watkins, President/Executive Director

California Alliance of African-American Educators

AFRICAN CHILDREN'S MANIFESTO

The Race to Re-Educate, Re-Tool and Empower Our Children

Lasha Pierce, M.D   Ajuana Black

Foreword and Contributing Author
Tovi Scruggs M.Ed.

First Edition

PUBLISHING COMPANY

Oakland, California

AFRICAN CHILDREN'S MANIFESTO
The Race to Re-Educate, Re-Tool and
Empower Our Children
by Lasha Pierce M.D. and Ajuana Black
Foreword by Tovi Scruggs M.Ed.

C/O Wise Woman HS Inc.
P.O. Box 27513
Oakland CA 94602

All rights reserved. No part of this book may be reproduced or transmitted in any form or by any means, electronic or mechanical, including photocopying, recording or by any information storage and retrieval system, without written permission from the author, except for the inclusion of brief quotations in a review.

Unattributed quotations are by Lasha Pierce, M.D.

Copyright © 2012 by Lasha Pierce, M.D.

ISBN 978-0-9888495-0-1

Printed in the United States of America

For Imani, Falating and Kitwana
the beautiful ones

Thank you for your
patience
forgiveness
and
understanding

Manifesto
Table of Contents

I. Foreword by Tovi Scruggs

II. Introduction

III. The Outer Circle- MacroCosm *Global Perspectives*

    1. Education as a Function of World View
    2. Euro-American Behaviorist Theory
    3. African World View
    4. Behavior and Discipline
    5. Community in Healing and Educating

IV. The Inner Circle- MicroCosm *Individual perspectives*

    6. Interview with Allen Scott Gordon, Public high school teacher

    7. JayVon Muhammad: National of Islam schools

    8. Interview with Kelly Clark, Public elementary school teacher

    9. Ajuana Black: Perspective of a home teacher

V. The Center- African Children's Manifesto *Our Children*

	10.	Tovi Scruggs M.Ed.: How to Be a Parent Champion
	11.	Call to Action
	12.	African Children's Manifesto
	13.	Introduction to Live Interviews with African American Males
VI.	**Appendices**	
VII.	***Footnotes and* References**	

A recording of Live Interviews can be viewed at our website

http://africanchildrensmanifesto.webs.com/.

Table of Contents

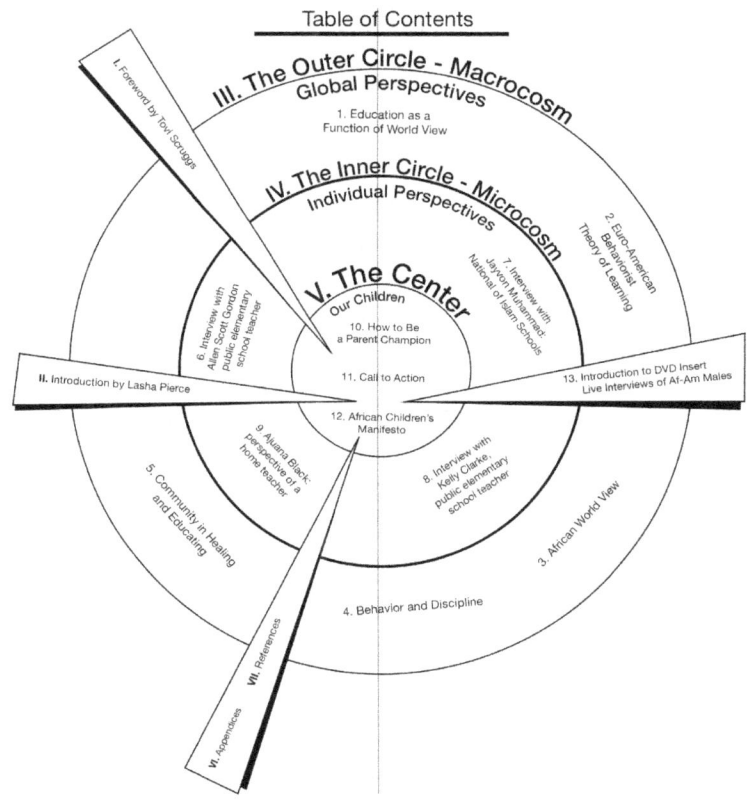

- I. Foreword by Toyi Scruggs
- II. Introduction by Lasha Pierce
- **III. The Outer Circle - Macrocosm**
  Global Perspectives
  1. Education as a Function of World View
  2. Euro-American Behaviorist Theory of Learning
  3. African World View
  4. Behavior and Discipline
  5. Community in Healing and Educating
- **IV. The Inner Circle - Microcosm**
  Individual Perspectives
  6. Interview with Allen Scott Gordon, public elementary school teacher
  7. Interview with Jayson Muhammed, National of Islam Schools
  8. Interview with Kelly Clarke, public elementary school teacher
  9. Aluana Black: perspective of a home teacher
- **V. The Center**
  Our Children
  10. How to Be a Parent Champion
  11. Call to Action
  12. African Children's Manifesto
  13. Introduction to DVD Insert Live Interviews of Af-Am Males
- VI. Appendices
- VII. References

I. FOREWORD

"If you are thinking one year ahead, sow seed. If you are thinking 10 years ahead, plant a tree. If you are thinking 100 years ahead, educate the people."
- Kuan Tzu, Chinese Poet

We all want our children to succeed. This book, this manifesto, is a testament to that desire. *African Children's Manifesto* is also a testament to the tenacity, collaboration, and creativity that exists in the hearts of many parents and educators.

I am humbled and honored to salute Dr. Lasha Pierce and Ajuana Black for the vision, courage, and determination to carry out the charge that dwells in their hearts and, wholeheartedly, I join their call to action to bring our community back to the larger conversation of how education is often failing our children. We - the adults, the educators, the parents, the leaders - are being beckoned by our children to not fail them too, but to take a stand and to take action to chaperone them on their educational journeys, hand in hand.

Highly disproportionate data and statistics that speak to the plight of African-American children in our current educational systems exist across the school continuum, starting with our very young boys who are being expelled as early as preschool. The trend of disproportionality continues through their completion of high school with standardized test results determining that, after more than 10 years in classrooms, over 55% of our teens are less-than-proficient in math and less-than-proficient in English. (To highlight the depth of that particular problem, African-American youth are often outscored by second language learners.) Further, institutional patterns across the nation exemplify that African-American youth are referred out of class, suspended, and expelled at rates two to three times higher than enrollment. Rather than inundate you further with data and statistics that have been prolific for over three decades, I choose instead to focus my energy on the antecedents of our educational epidemic. Only when we confront the precursors of mindsets, conversations, and actions can we best address and heal them with lasting, transformational solutions.

Part of my intention in contributing to *African Children's Manifesto* is to avoid repetition of the important points authored and shared about our African and African-American cultures, our history, and much of the complexities that our African-American children face in Euro-dominated schools and school systems. My goal in this work is to present solid strategies, tools, and supports to empower parents to best serve African American youth to survive, thrive, and achieve in our educational systems.

While the common symbol for education is an apple, there is a significant irony of a little black boy on *African Children's Manifesto*'s cover clutching the lemons that are the fruits of his labor with an innocent smile of his "job well done." Of course, we can think of the old cliché, "When life gives you lemons, make lemonade," but that would be too easy- too predictable. I say that the irony of the lemons is truly the gift of what our ancestral heritage has done all too well in this country: taken an acidic environment and generated an alkaline state in order to delay a more rapid decline from high levels of acidity. Interestingly, both the processes of "acid to alkaline" and "lemons to lemonade" create additional work, when all we really want is to take the sweetness of education and thrive from the start. In our current educational system, others get apples – clean, crisp, sweet apples that nourish while we are forced to tolerate and accept lemons. Our children, while young, will accept the lemons given to them as good enough, but as time goes on, they will recognize the differences, obvious and otherwise, between apples and lemons. Our children are not served fully as our current schools stand, and they are caught in the race to re-educate, re-tool, and empower. It is a race that is almost futile unless we take a greater stand as a community and - as adults, educators, leaders, and parents - to fully partner with schools and take more significant and active roles in our children's education.

Currently, we have to fight and cajole to simply get a base level of education while others do not. It is incumbent upon us to be more strategic, systemic, and united in this fight. Dr. Pierce and Ms. Black are calling on our community. Join the call.

It is critical that we unify as a community to take the lead in propelling our children to success. This must first begin in our homes and translate to our own institutions for our children that reflect the values and love that we have for our children. No other community is more vested in the success and achievement of our own children than we are; we must act like it and align our actions and choices to support our children's fruitfulness as though the future of our race depends on it. Because, in fact, it does. We must take action in the education of our children with greater intentionality, clarity, and strategy.

I know what it looks like and what it takes to make these grandiose statements of action. In 1997, I was a high school teacher walking out of a staff meeting where we were discussing test scores of "those students." "Those students" were the African-American students who were being taught by a predominantly Euro-American staff- a progressive and highly-skilled staff who genuinely cared about all of the students yet could not bridge the cultural disconnect creating the concerns. The more time I spent in the school and around these conversations, the more my spirit ached.

One day, the pain got so great that God relieved it with a vision, a vision of change for African-American students and our greater community. The groundwork of the vision began and, after years of planning, the vision manifested. In 2002, a dear friend and I began a thriving educational oasis intentionally designed for African-American youth in grades 6 – 12: ASA Academy and Community Science Center ("ah-sah"). There was no achievement gap at ASA. We did our work in excellence for over seven years, sending graduates to colleges all over the nation. We closed in 2009 due to the economic downturn and the lack of philanthropy during that time. The loss of ASA left a loss in our community; however, the lives that ASA touched have been forever enhanced, mine included.

It was the dream and vision of ASA that has catapulted me into a deeper understanding of our community and the needs to heal our own psychosis as it relates to true unity (beyond lip-service and cultural events), as well as the imperative to put the needs of our children before our own. It is because of ASA that I was able to formulate and create educational strategies and practices that validate my beliefs of how the home and school must be tightly connected for the ultimate success of our children. It is because of ASA that I know how to identify and create powerful academic school culture that is palpable and facilitates transformational achievement. It is because of ASA that I have forged relationships with powerful, dynamic "parent champions" that delay their own gratification and educate their children with an attitude of "by any means necessary."

Ironically, it is because of ASA that I have developed into the educational leader that I continue to become as I serve thousands under my current principalship. I am centered, focused, and knowing in the strength of my gifts and vision to do what was at the core of the initial vision: to create a model school that meets the needs of African-American youth (and all youth) beyond test scores and close the academic and racial achievement gaps with the populations it affects most.

It is critical that we heed the teachings of *African Children's Manifesto* and unify to develop educational alternatives for our children: demand higher standards and results from our schools: participate more fully in the realization of those results: serve as contributing authors of the agendas in our schools: and take more definitive action in our homes.

I express deep gratitude to Lasha and Ajuana for inviting my voice to be included in *African Children's Manifesto*, to be deemed "expert" in some way. I give ultimate gratitude to God, My Most High, My Alpha and Omega, for breathing into me a purpose and vision in the larger work of education to serve our children, lead and inspire fellow educators, and create Parent Champions™ for the greater good of our children's success for generations to come.

Thinking 100 years ahead on behalf of us all -
Tovi Scruggs, M.Ed.
Visionary & Educational Leader
Oakland, CA - December 2012

II. INTRODUCTION

This book began its gestation over 20 years ago, before birthing my three children. When I decided to become a mother, I had no idea that I had also decided to become a teacher. A child's first teachers are her or his parents. I did my best to learn from my own mother and father, aunties and uncles, grandmothers and grandfathers and women and men in the community how best to fulfill the duties of both parenting and teaching. I read books and compared notes with other parents, who themselves were by definition teachers as well. We all had varying levels of information, but shared it freely and often. I am grateful for my education from the wider community of African women and men. From within the womb and beyond, the education of my children has been a constant process of both affirmation and discovery.

Being an educator has been full of delight, surprise and power. The quest to teach my children not only the things that I know and value, but also how to learn from experience, the universe, and ultimately oneself has led us all to heights and depths we cherish. However, I was soon to realize that not all educators of my children would be filled with the same sense of delight or duty. Not all educational systems would have at their core the intention of enlightening or empowering my children.

It is worth mentioning a few terms here that I use in the body of this book. I try to avoid terms like "Black" and "White" when describing people, culture or philosophy. Those words describe colors and are too small to attempt to describe the origin, history, or depth of an entire group of people. I choose to describe people in terms of geographical and cultural origin: thus you will notice the terms African and European. I also combine those prefixes with American, as the subject of this book is the education system in America. When speaking of worldview, I try to reveal that depending on the historical and cultural origin, people will see things in the world differently. Values may differ, and what is considered acceptable behavior will differ.

In a world and time where the European worldview is dominant, education has become (at least for children in America, Europe or other countries influenced by either) a tool for industry and technology, stripped of its universal essence. The emphasis in education is on those skills that allow you to build bigger factories or make more electronic gadgets. Tying a student's education to the good of others, the planet, or even themselves in the form of art or music is lacking. Practical skills to learn community building, tradesman-ship, business and commerce are lacking. Critical thinking is not rewarded, nor is it taught. I would even go as far as saying that education even outside of America and Europe in countries where industry and technology are not necessarily the driving force, is merely a tool for maintaining some other system, whether it be a political system, an economic system, or religious system. That alone is no crisis. All societies use education as a tool to fuel the engine that is itself. That is, all societies must train their members to keep the society going strong and in an agreed upon direction. Even those varying cultures that make up the subtext of the greater society can and often find ways of scripting supplemental educational goals in line with their particular set of values- values that go beyond the practical necessities of economics.

An example would be the Chinese sub-culture in America and how many Chinese students are expected to attend special "Chinese schools" on weekends and after the traditional school day. This ensures that in addition to the technologically rich education they get in traditional American schools, the students would also learn Chinese culture, language, culture and values. Similarly, "Hebrew schools" exist for Jewish students in America.

It is clear that many in the African-American (AA) community find value in also receiving the traditional American education. Indeed, it is practical and needed in many cases to achieve financial success. It helps to keep the societal engine running. However, within the AA community, the disconnect between those that are invested in maintaining American society as a whole as it is, and those who are not invested in keeping things as they are, has created a wide gap within our own community. We are either very successful or painfully unsuccessful, and the middle is shrinking. What of those students who need more than what is offered to be happy, successful and whole? For this particular examination of education, I will exclude those who have successfully navigated our educational system and thus fueled the industrial and technological aspects of American society and who have mastered the vehicles to keep them successful as defined by our society.

Instead, I will explore larger questions: How can we provide a meaningful education to those who struggle both internally and externally with the European-American (EA) educational model as it now stands? What are our educational models that fuel the alternative, parallel multi-verse? Can and should we script educational goals for ourselves that both address practical economic goals, but also develop culturally appropriate values unique to our experience?

It is no secret that many African-American children, especially our young males, have not faired well under the Euro-American educational system. By extension, I would also dare to theorize that African children throughout all former European colonies don't fair much better either. I could be wrong. I recently heard a staggering statistic about Oakland, California (where I live) placing the high school drop out rate among African-American children upward of 40%. When African-American males were isolated as a group the rate approached 50%! That's half of our children in Oakland not completing high school. Nationally, the numbers are not much better. This statistic tells me one thing: that the educational objectives of the public school system have become, at best, irrelevant to our youth and, at worst, destructive. There has been extensive research in the education literature describing the "achievement gap" between European-American children versus African-American children. Some researchers have even attempted to offer some explanations: differing poverty levels, educational levels of the families, nuclear versus single parent households, etc. I would like to suggest we spend more time extensively exploring the fundamental question of cultural-relevance: both from the standpoint of African versus European worldview and philosophy and the practical intentions and applications of education.

    My own children have experienced different educational models throughout their early formative years up through high school. They have attended private European-American schools, private African-American schools, been home schooled, and attended public schools as well as charter schools. They have not attended religious schools or boarding schools, so my direct experience is lacking in those areas. The charter schools were a series of unintended social experiments and varied from predominantly African-American students and staff, to predominantly European-American students and staff, to predominantly Hispanic students and European-American staff to predominantly African-American students and European-American staff. The charter combination that served them best was when the students **and staff** (including teachers and administrators) were predominantly African-American. The private school combination that served them best was when students **and staff** (including teachers and administrators) were predominantly African-American. They thrived under my instruction at homeschool: a decidedly African-American immersion as well. At varying times their education in

European-American schools, whether public or private, wavered between "thriving" (rarely but sometimes) to "drowning," with most times being in the middle spectrum of "tolerating" or "surviving." In those instances, the environments were so full of mental stress that I dare say little learning was occurring and I, as a proactive parent, had to improve their educational experience by changing their educational environment (several times) as well as supplementing their education at home.

As I have befriended other African-American parents over my adult years and chronicled their struggle to educate their children, this theme of our children being better educated from within our own African-American community schools is a common one among us. Why is it that many of our children thrive in our own institutions but struggle in others? Is this because schools serving African-American youth have a less rigorous curriculum? Is it because the children are unable to function across racial lines? The answer to these viable questions is "No." Having been privy to a variety of different schools, classrooms and styles, I have the ability to compare schools on many different fronts. Not only can I say that the African- American schools which my children attended had curricula as rigorous (in some cases more rigorous) as the European-American schools in the area at the time, but they also had social and cultural qualities that soared above those of their European-American counterparts.

African-American schools (where the teachers and administrators are AA) that my children attended had higher standards of accountability (to self, family, community, the cosmos): more informed and humane standards of discipline: and also maintained a sense of family, community, respect and belonging. The staff members, as well as the parent and student bodies were extensions of me: we come from the same culture, with the same values and expectations. We shared the same love, aspirations for and knowledge of our children. We shared the same language and communication, both verbal and non-verbal. In contrast, my experience with European-American schools has been one of alienation and isolation. My children are not a part of the EA community, and thus were "alien" to the dominant culture. No acknowledgement of cross-cultural differences existed, nor any admission of the need for staff members to receive cultural competence training. Although my children (like most others) could navigate the racial diversity of the other children with ease, the power dynamic between adult European-American teachers and administrators (complete with all their stereotypes, prejudices, cultural ignorance and in some cases fear and hostility) and African-American children was a whole other undertaking. Accountability was to a test, a school policy, or Euro-centric values. Discipline tended to be exclusionary (suspension or expulsion) or confinement (detention), which is likely a descendant of slave discipline and a cousin of current prison practices. My children did not voice these as concerns or challenges, nor did they have to. Their education suffered, and at times their self-esteem buckled under such a psychologically violent and unwelcoming system.

    This cycle is not uncommon to other African-American children as well. In my circle of African-American women and men friends with children, we have all at some time or another experienced similar challenges to educating our children under this educational system with a Euro-dominant worldview. Moreover, the African-American women and men whom I've had the pleasure of learning from and exchanging parenting styles with, like myself, are educated, not impoverished, and are highly motivated in ensuring the success of their children. Most were married and all are either educators themselves or healthcare providers. We have all self-taught our children, volunteered at schools, participated in the PTA, actively sought out partnerships with our children's schools and teachers, donated time and resources and any other strategy you might imagine that parents of "successful" students would do. We demand excellence, high moral character and responsibility among our children. We actively involve our children in extra-curricular and after school programs. We seek out tutors, mentors and community advocates when necessary. We immerse our children in the arts, athletics, cultural activities and spirituality. But despite our best efforts, some of our children do not thrive in the Euro-American educational system.

Remember, education is necessarily good at promoting the values of the dominant culture, which in this case is European-American. My intention is not to waste precious time and energy proposing ways to change the public school systems all over the nation. Rather I postulate ways that we, in our own worldview, with what we deem practical and necessary, can redefine our goals of education for our children as well as redefine the best ways of achieving those goals, whether within the current system or without. Many private African-American institutions of learning have been successful in doing just that. However, not many of us in the AA community can afford to pay for private education, and many of the private AA schools are not sustainable for this very reason. One of the most effective schools I've ever experienced here in Oakland, ASA Academy and Community Science Center, had to close its doors due, in part, to financial crisis. Others have been successful in remaining viable options in the community, but still struggle to do so.

Once we collectively do the work of studying what our children need to gain most in the educational system, we can approach that system with concrete solutions, suggestions and, eventually, demands. We can also take the lead in developing alternate educational settings for our children that are affordable, sustainable and productive.

The following pages will take you on a journey into the minds and lives of ordinary African-American men and women; trekking across the dry plains of education in search of water for our children. May your thirst be quenched when you arrive with us at the water's edge.

III. THE OUTER CIRCLE-MACROCOSM

Education as a Function of World View

In its technical sense, education is the process by which society deliberately transmits its accumulated knowledge, skills and values from one generation to another. There are then a few questions that beg to be asked.

The act of transmitting presumes a form of successful communication between the one with the knowledge and the one in search of it. Let's assume that knowledge is a universal value. The *form* the knowledge takes however and the ways it may be transmitted are not. Additionally, skill sets and their relative value certainly vary according to culture. In a perfect world, the umbrella of "American" culture would be enough to set a standard for forms of knowledge, how knowledge is transmitted, what skills are considered mandatory and what values should be embraced. We do know, though, that America is fat with a variety of sub-cultures, the most ubiquitous being African-American. To begin to grasp what this may mean for the education of our youth, let's examine the evolution of education in our history.

Classical African societies such as Kemet give us some clues as to how education was used by our ancestors. Most boys learned the craft of their fathers; for example the son of a baker would learn the skills necessary to become a baker. Girls learned from their mothers skills such as cooking and child-rearing. People holding civic positions needed to learn math, and likewise reading and writing was necessary for scribes and priests. Children of royalty (both genders) enjoyed a comprehensive education including reading and writing, history, math, astronomy, music, geography, science and medicine. Education for the most part held a very practical purpose for most people. Even something as seemingly abstract as astronomy helped the society to predict weather cycles and the swell of the Nile for planting and agricultural purposes. Most classical African civilizations had similar practical uses of education. African societies that later embraced Christianity or Islam later went on to incorporate the study of those religious teachings as part of requisite education as well.

Although there were multitudes of African civilizations that thrived between the times of ancient Kemet and the present time, contemporary education of African-Americans is most visibly shaped by the brutality of African enslavement in the Americas. The term MAAFA (*mah-off-ah*) pertains to the historic Trans-Atlantic African slave trade. It is derived from a Swahili term meaning "disaster, terrible occurrence or great tragedy." The African MAAFA ushered in a new era of education for captured African prisoners of war. No matter the destination, be it the North, South, Central Americas or the Caribbean, formal education was forbidden as a tactic for continued oppression. The quest for education became at once taboo and dangerous. Yet, informal education was hidden in plain site. Africans passed down skills to each other and their children about how to grow and maintain plants (many native to mother Africa), taught African history, how to prepare traditional African cuisine, hair-care, midwifery, herbology, fashion, music and dance. We taught each other the gods and goddesses of our mothers, as well as basic astronomy (later used as a tool of navigation for fugitive sea travel and during the underground railroad in America). Again, as in our history, education was practical in every sense. Here in North America, the need to attain freedom also made the urgency to learn to speak, read and write English reveal itself, despite the latter two often being the source of punishment, torture and even death. Of course in other locations, the dominant European language varied and included Spanish, Portuguese, French or Dutch. It is at this point that our interface with the pathology of Euro-American psyche gives birth to our very troubled relationship around being educated by a system created by and for the advancement of Euro-American people, often at our own expense.

To preserve some morsel of sanity, we started to create our own schools of formal education here in North America in the mid-1800's. The agreed upon reason throughout history was that we were forced to create our schools due to by being excluded from the Euro-centric schools. That may have some validity, but I believe that some of us would have made this choice regardless, as many of us make an effort to do so today even without the rules of segregation. African-American schools sprouted like wildflowers in an open field of earth and sun. The focus of some was agriculture, while others were a broader liberal studies focus. Many had curricula in Ancient African civilizations and African psychology, subjects not widely offered at Euro-American schools. Still some offered classes seen in traditional Euro-American schools like English, Business and a variety of non-English European languages. This was our educational hybridization in its infancy. By the 1950s, the struggle to integrate the Euro-American schools in the United States prevailed. Sit-ins, riots, strikes and marches marked this time in our resurrection. But another, more quiet revolution was to come. In the 1960s and 1970s the resurgence of the private African-American school was evident; this time by desire not force. The Black Power movement gave us pride and ownership over the education of our children. In addition to the skills necessary to be successful in Euro-America, we wanted our children to have the knowledge of themselves and their people, knowledge of our ancestors. We wanted our children to look upon these things with their own lenses and not those of another people. We made a conscious attempt to return to African based values, philosophy and worldview.

Euro-American education has also evolved over time. The emergence of secondary education in the United States did not happen until 1910, caused by the rise in big businesses and technological advances in factories (for instance, the emergence of electrification), that required skilled workers. In order to meet this new job demand, high schools were created and the curriculum focused on practical job skills that would better prepare students for white-collar or skilled blue-collar work. In other words, the goal of Euro-education at the time was to fuel the technological revolution.

In economic terms, this equates to providing labor for business owners. This logic still stands today. The goal of secondary education is to prepare students for college, earn a college degree and go on to land a "good paying job" (laboring for another). If you fail to achieve the goal of college, you are likely to land in a service position (laboring for another with much less pay), the military (killing and dying for another) or potentially a position of crime (ending up in "detention" and often laboring for another in exchange for your freedom). Some in our society are even regulated to a position of invisibility; not seen by society or even by oneself or community as a valuable, productive entity. An example of this would be those who have soft skills that are difficult to market and exploit like community artists, griots, farmers, political and social activists, and even some educators. Productivity is seen only in the economic sense. There are some exclusive, private Euro-American schools that prepare students for entrepreneurship -- actually learning to be the "other" that the rest of society is working for. However, it goes without saying that this is the road less traveled and reserved for the elite.

As the focus of education was becoming more "skill" oriented in nature, many in the educational circles of Euro-American academia began to analyze the validity of the metamorphosis of the goals of formal education. The Euro-American educational model had reached a crossroads. In his chapter "Evaluation of a Character Education Curriculum" author Campbell comments in the book *Education for Values,*

    Since the 1960's teacher education has downplayed the teacher's role as a transmitter of social and personal values and emphasized other areas such as teaching techniques, strategies, models, and skills. More and more the vision of a good teacher is as the good technician, the skilled craftsman, who has acquired those behavioral skills and strategies that the "effective teacher" research claims are related to achievement. However, the fact that "effective" is defined as the students' scores on standardized tests of basic skills, but without reference to higher-order intellectual processes or concern about the students' morals, is of concern to many parents and educators. Educational psychology, rather than philosophy and religion, has become the basis of teacher training. In most cases, educational psychology focuses on the individual, separated from the social context. Additionally, modern education has been heavily influenced by the behavioral approach, which has proved adept at developing instructional methods that impact achievement as measured by standardized tests. In the opinion of most researchers in the area of character and moral development, additional emphasis must be placed on the philosophical "why" of education in addition to the technical "how." [1]

    Two themes jump out in the above passage. The first revelation is that Euro-American researchers are having an internal dialogue about the turn their education has taken in recent history away from character development. The

---

1 Campbell

second revelation is that even if there is a push toward this moral and character development (presumably via philosophy and religion from the authors above references) it is not likely to service the needs of our children any better than the current system. Why is this? Because, as you will see later, the fundamental philosophy of African peoples is dialectically opposed to that of Euro-American philosophy. In addition, it is deep in one's worldview where concepts of character and religion are born. We also mentioned earlier that to educate successfully, there must be an effective and agreed upon vehicle of communication, something that can vary among differing cultures. To get a clearer understanding of how the educational system applies the overarching backdrop of the dominant culture, we need to examine the concept of the behavioral approach to education as Campbell mentions.

Euro-American Behaviorist Theory of Learning

According to the behaviorists, learning can be defined as the relatively permanent change in behavior brought about as a result of experience or practice.[2]

The focus of the behavioral approach is on how the environment impacts overt behavior. The only way we know what is going on in the mind, according to most behaviorists, is to look at outward behavior. There are three types of behavioristic learning theories:

1. Contiguity -- any stimulus and response connected in time and/or space will tend to be associated (a baseball player wearing a certain pair of socks on the day he hits three home runs; a student making a good grade on a test after trying several different study techniques)
2. Classical (Respondent) Conditioning -- association of stimuli (an antecedent stimulus will reflexively elicit an innate emotional or physiological response; another stimulus will elicit an orienting response).
3. Operant (Instrumental) Conditioning -- connection of emitted behavior and its consequences (reinforcement and punishment)

Behavior is one's actions in relation to environment, which includes other beings as well as the physical environment. It is one's outward response to various stimuli, whether internal or external, conscious or subconscious, overt or covert, and voluntary or involuntary. For example, a baby crying is a behavior that could be in response to an injury (an external stimulus), hunger (an internal stimulus) or a varying number of other stimuli. The stimulus, or "reason"

---

[2] Huitt

for the behavior may be obvious to those observing or may not be obvious. In the case of the African-American student, obvious stimuli such as financial and/or educational resources will be recognized by the dominant Euro-American educational system. Students recognized as being poor, often referred to as "under privileged", will be assumed to be doing poorly in school due to lack of money to buy food or school supplies. Invisible forces such as racism, psychological hostility and cultural indifference will be missed as determinants of behavior. A student who is not engaged in classroom lessons or seems uninterested will almost certainly NOT be assumed to be suffering racism or hostility at the hands of the school or teacher. He or she will be more likely to be assumed to be of low intelligence, have a mental disorder or have a problem with drug or alcohol use.

In addition, it will be lost on the ignorant observer that different students will be experiencing different stimuli, and therefore behaviors cannot be reliably compared between groups of students. For example, students holding American citizenship do not experience the same social rejection that a recent immigrant child might. Children with foreign language accents may find that they are ridiculed by students who can speak English more readily. The racial profiling that African-American males experience both in the criminal justice system and the educational system is not experienced by their Euro-American counterparts. The chronic stress caused by constantly being the object of suspicion, the assumption by others that African-American males lack intelligence or ambition, among other invisible hostilities can breed apathy, anger and mistrust, which can be interpreted by the educator as sloth, behavioral challenges, or lack of intelligence. Thus, behaviors of the learner are only interpreted within the limited knowledge base and "pathologic personality" of the instructor. Here, instructor is used to represent the Euro-American educational model as a whole.

Real Life Examples:

Example 1- Student is asked in private why he seems to consistently have difficulty following the direction of an administrator. His response, "He treats us like we are all these poor, deprived, fatherless kids. I have a Daddy. He's not my Daddy."

Here, the above mentioned treatment was the administrator assuming that the African-American males needed more "discipline" and thus constantly taking a tone with the group that was ultimately deemed offensive. In his attempt to reject the (what the student felt was unjustified) surrogate "parent," the student also rejected all other instruction, even what related to his education.

Example 2- After a review of vocabulary words to prepare a class of 11th graders for the SAT, the teacher says, "You should try to use these words in your everyday life, it will make you *seem* smarter."

This is an example of psychological violence. The teacher was of European origin and the entire class population was African-American. The suggestion that the students are not smart at all, but that if they speak more like him they will at least seem smart is a blatant insult which degrades the entire group of students while summarily rejecting their culture, form of expression and intellectual ability. The stimuli experienced by the student(s) in these examples (disrespect, pity, and condescension among others) may not be recognized by the educator or administrator as such and thus the behavioral response elicited (anger, frustration, defiance, mistrust) can easily be misinterpreted as behavioral non-compliance or even academic inferiority.

Euro-American education uses classical and operant conditioning frequently. It appears to have been born even before education was formalized in the American society, as we see it in conditioning of captured, enslaved Africans early in European and American history, and in the industrial-prison complex where many African-American citizens find themselves today. No matter which behavioral learning theory is applied, learning is *implied* by behavior. For example, one's understanding of a taught concept would be implied by one's performance on a standardized or written test. This measures a finite behavior, void of it's cultural or societal context, and thus a false measurement altogether. It ignores unseen stimuli that may influence the behavior, as discussed before. Grades are assigned based on "correct" and "incorrect" answers even in subjects where right and wrong can be subjective depending on the world view or cultural context. Remember, the historical African education was practical,relevant and had a beneficial purpose; a purpose born in the necessities of the community at large. Oral communication was valued as well as written communication. Hands-on demonstration of mastery was necessary at other times. A small example of how this may play out in contemporary education would be the student who is unmotivated to complete an assignment or prepare for an exam due to his or her inability to see the relevance to his or her life. We see countless students fall victim to irrelevant, culturally incompetent curricula and who then achieve at suboptimal levels.

African Worldview

The European world view is far superior to the others in its ability to generate material accumulation, technological efficiency, and imperial might. That does not make it universal. [3] It places much value on the material, so much so that the quest to acquire and control it becomes the driving life principle. In contrast, an African worldview places value on the spirit. It honors the unseen. It honors emotion. It does not seek to conquer and control, but seeks harmony with what is. In the outstanding work by Marimba Ani, *Yurugu, An African-Centered Critique of European Cultural Thought and Behavior,* Ani decisively makes this case:

> This idea of control is facilitated by first separating the human being into distinct compartments ("principles"). Plato distinguishes the compartments of "reason" and "appetite" or "emotion". Reason is a higher principle, in opposition to the other [emotion]. The superiority of the intellect over the emotional self is established as spirit is separated from matter. ...Once the "person" was artificially split into conflicting faculties or tendencies, it made sense [to the European mind] to think in terms of one faculty "winning" or controlling the other(s). It is this very "split" perception of reality that European controlling, imperialistic behavior depends. (p.32)

Consider for a moment the implications this might have on American educational philosophy. The dominant Euro-culture in America has essentially accepted the view that individuals are fragmented, not whole beings. The system is made up of a perpetual lever that is always off

---

[3] Ani

balance, or full of "fragmented" educators attempting to educate "whole" students. Taken a step further, the "fragmented" educators have even placed categorical importance of some fragments over others, and the students whom operate in a more balanced way can be and often are penalized for not splitting their psyche and having one half of themselves dominate the other. This is not to say that individual educators do this purposely or with malicious intent. This is the result of the root Euro-American philosophy having dominion over a very diverse and increasingly non-Euro-American student body. Ani goes on to say:

> What Plato seems to have done is to have laid a rigorously constructed foundation for the repudiation of the symbolic sense- the denial of cosmic, intuitive knowledge. It is this process that we need to trace, this development in formative European thought which was eventually to have had such a devastating effect on the nontechnical aspects of the culture. It led to the materialization of the universe as conceived by the European mind- a materialization that complemented and supported the intense psycho-cultural need for control of the self and others. (p.30)

It is this very denial of intuitive knowledge that allows for witch hunts in Salem, fear of the occult, and destruction of our planet. This also makes the education of our children very limited in scope and emotionally challenging. Education is limited to the material. Those who are most successful in this system have the very unique and evolved ability to interchange between the two worldviews - a complex skill indeed. For those who find this difficult, the results can be evident in poor academic performance within the Euro-American educational system.

Friedrich Juenger said "being" is good, valued and intelligent (static). "Becoming" is devalued, inferior, irrational" (movement). If the African worldview, which values motion and cooperation is devalued by the dominant worldview of the educational system, then being motivated to improve and striving toward excellence becomes difficult. The idea that those who are already successful are superior to those striving to become successful creates a permanent achievement gap and promotes a dichotomy of thought and action. The successful continue to perform well and the quest of those students who are less successful to improve is not valued or rewarded. Stasis is seen as superior to motion. Individuality is superior to relating to the group. This is in direct contradiction to nature and the cosmos, and creates an unnatural conflict in the psyche of the "whole" African child. Ani adds:

"Norms" are rules of conduct that specify what should and should not be done. The "normative aspects of culture" combine to form a set of of guidelines by which people regulate their own behavior and that of [others]. Robin Williams was quoted here from <u>American Society</u>.

"So that 'values' and 'norms' as they are used here can only be supported or positively 'sanctioned' within the culture in such a way that behavior that conforms to them is 'rewarded'- meets with 'success' and 'approval'- while behavior that contradicts them is 'punished'-results in 'failure' and is 'put-down' by [society] or is simply not rewarded in any way, i.e. not recognized as 'valued' behavior." (p.337)

The double-edged sword of the Euro-American educational system for African-American children in the United States is deadly. It can result in a spiritual and emotional death of sorts. The dull side carves the spirit with fragmented psycho-pathology and a cloak of invisibility that veils the values of the African worldview. The sharp side slices even the most resilient with what Ani calls a "rhetorical ethic" and "cultural violence".

The rhetorical ethic is made possible by the fact that hypocrisy as a mode of behavior is a valued theme in European life; the same hypocritical behavior that its presence sanctions. Again, "value" refers to that which is encouraged and approved in a culture. European culture is constructed in such a way that successful survival within it discourages honesty and directness and encourages dishonesty and deceit - the ability to appear to be something other than what one is; to hide one's "self," one's motives and intent. (p.316)

Failure to master this critical skill can be catastrophic. Becoming fluent in Euro-American worldview and ethics is necessary to thrive in its educational system and thus society, but can come at a large spiritual and emotional cost if one is not careful. It is necessary to become a master of deceit to be materially successful, but also maintain one's African ethic to be spiritually whole. The dominant culture which sanctions stealing, bullying, raping, murdering and lying with it's very actions (both in its bloody history and current foreign and domestic policies) can at once stand in judgment of a student's behavior in the educational system and enforce dreadful consequences to those who dare to mimic the monster's display. Ani continues:

The capacity of one cultural group to commit acts of physical brutality and destruction against another is proportionate to the place of power (i.e. control over "other") in its ideology and the degree to which its image and conception of those outside the culture lack the characteristics of "humanness." European culture has an enormous capacity for the perpetration of physical violence against other cultures; its integrity is neither threatened nor disrupted by such occurrences. The physical body may be critical to the maintenance of human existence, but the quality of that existence depends very much on our mental and spiritual condition. First World cultures tend to be spiritually oriented, and therefore cultural violence (ideological and psychological) is at least as damaging to their humanity as is physical violence. (p. 427).

Here we see how the position of power within Euro-American ideology and its need to control can surface pathologically within the educational model. Euro-American behavior historically has been aggressive, impulsive, narcissistic and lacking empathy- traits that are considered psychological ailments at best. The European American worldview embraces violence as a means to control others and has been made manifest over and over in the volumes of history. Every continent on the Earth has been under the subjection of European rule, destruction, and desolation. When liberation movements across the globe put Europe on her heels, she was successful in maintaining enough military presence and control in key regions to satisfy her psychopathology. Educational curricula have been challenged within the Euro-American system to decrease negative stereotypes of different cultural groups in teaching materials, be more inclusive of non-dominant cultures, and promote multiculturalism. However, the absence of physical violence should not overshadow the presence of continued ideological and psychological violence. This deformed relationship between the ethic starved, fragmented educator attempting to educate the ethic rich, whole student drives the unspoken, often even unrecognized inner conflict many African-American students find themselves with. Let me demonstrate how this plays out.

Take for example the typical, European American. Whether he or she is a politician, police officer, member of the school board, authors textbooks, is an administrator or teacher in a school or even a journalist who helps to shape public opinion, the European American world view has a direct impact on what is taught and how it is taught in the schools. If the European world view values control, material accumulation and imperial might, then all laws, policies, curricula, books and images will serve to glorify those values. Thus, it is expected that African-American students, who don't necessarily share those values, would still be expected to be controlled, manipulated for material wealth and agreeable to being "conquered". Don't question authority. Learn only those skills necessary to make money. Only speak when told to, to one person at a time. Don't show too much emotion or passion when interacting with "authority" figures in the system. Hide all remnants of your culture and language. Speak proper English. Dress in proper European attire (suit and tie). A show of resistance to any of those values, such as having independent thought and action, not holding all allegiance to the material, and/or asserting sovereignty as a free and worthy human, all have the potential to create a backlash of punishment and consequences. Speaking in class (without permission) can be punishable with removal from the classroom. Questioning "authority" can end in the same, or, worse, incarceration. African-American males with braids and/or beards are stereotyped, feared and treated aggressively. The same is true if your speech holds patterns of African roots ("Ebonics").

Bobby Wright, an African psychologist, says that the European pattern of behavior is symptomatic of the "psychopathic personality," who [among other things] is unable to learn from experience, has almost no ethical development, has total disregard for appropriate patterns of behavior and rejects constituted authority.(Ani P.449-450) This is the absolutely insane psychological environment our children find themselves in when we assign their education to the Euro-American paradigm.

Behavior and Discipline

In order for someone to judge if another person is behaving well, that someone would have to know what defines good behavior. There would need to be agreement between the parties that a shared standard had not been met. Behavior is rooted in one's culture. We have discussed that the fundamental values of African peoples compared to those of European peoples do not match. Therefore, our youth find themselves measured again and again by a foreign cultural and behavioral standard that they often reject. This is a strain on the psyche. It is a strain on self-confidence, ideas of self-worth and ability. This disconnect creates a hostile environment for learning.

One of the most obvious areas of this psychological environment, where the standard of behavior is dictated by the European need to exercise power and exert control becomes most problematic as it pertains to our children's ability to achieve is in the area of behavior and discipline. The educational institutions made by those with "total disregard for appropriate patterns of behavior" as Bobby Wright describes them, are the same institutions which author appropriate patterns of behavior for our children. The culture responsible for educating our children has a pattern of "rejecting constituted authority." It is amazing how any of our children manage to wade through this swamp of psychological chaos. Indeed, many of our children succumb to the overpowering effects of such a diseased system. It is well documented that the disproportionate numbers of African-American students, males in particular, that are subjected to school discipline policies are linked to both school drop-out rates and the subsequent entry into the juvenile detention system. Failure to educate our children appropriately not only places them at academic and economic disadvantages, but also places them in danger of ultimately loosing their freedom, their humanity, and their very lives.

There is an overrepresentation of African-American males in both special education programs and in the application of exclusionary discipline policies in the United States. Exclusionary policies are those that remove the student from the learning environment, often with no recourse to re-visit missed lessons or material. It can include referrals out of class, school suspensions and school expulsions. When reviewing the literature examining disparities in discipline policies, the theme that floats to the surface is consistently that of "Cultural Conflict," that is the inability of the dominant culture to culturally reconcile with the needs of the learner.

Let's examine those behaviors that are considered "good" or acceptable in the Euro-American educational model (both academic and social) and discuss some of them in detail.

Behaviors	Positive	Negative
Academic	HIgh test scores	Low test scores
	Large volume written work	low volume written work
Social	Conform	Defiant
	Passive	Active
	Harmony	Disrupt

Behaviors that are assigned as "good" in the Euro-American educational paradigm are two tiered, depending on if one applies the term to the "other" or to a member of the Euro-American fraternity. Good "students" (slaves, employees or women all can be substituted here in the dominant paradigm) are passive and in harmony with the status quo-which is European dominance. They are conforming and avoid conflict. They sit still in upright chairs and desks without speaking unless called upon. They are silent, motionless individuals. They focus and complete one task at a time, in a linear fashion. They are STATIC. They reflect the Euro-American principle of control.

"Bad" students talk to other students. They talk without prompts or permission. They speak to be heard. They are questioning. They move their minds, bodies and mouths frequently. They are independent of remote control. They are active learners, engaging their surroundings, and forming active relationships with others. They multi-task and interact with multiple stimuli in a circular or spiral fashion. They are in MOTION. They reflect the African principle of harmony. Harmony is the simultaneous combination of tones. Sound requires motion. This is interpreted by the European-American paradigm as being "out of control". You can begin to see how the dominant ideas about behavior and discipline in the Euro-American educational model can be challenging and even damaging to the African personality.

In the the journal, <u>Exceptional Children</u>, author Dr. Brenda Townsend touches on this theme in her article, "The Disproportionate Discipline of African-American Learners: Reducing School Suspensions and Expulsions." She discusses how cultural conflicts may pose threats to African-American students' participation and engagement in schools. For example, many African-American students are accustomed to engaging in multiple activities simultaneously in their homes and communities. They can be involved in multiple conversations while eating, studying, watching television, or participating in other recreational activities. Thus, those students may prefer activities that allow them to socialize with others while completing tasks. At school, teachers usually expect and reward students' individual engagement in one activity at a time, as opposed to managing multiple tasks and working with others. If school instructional goals are primarily structured to promote working on one activity at a time, students may be penalized for their need and ability to simultaneously engage in multiple activities, being perceived as willfully ignoring directions or as being otherwise insubordinate. She goes on to describe how African-American students' task orientations may also conflict with mainstream school culture. "According to Gilbert and Gay (1985), African-American students have a propensity toward 'stage-setting' behaviors before actually beginning tasks. Toward this end, they may execute behavioral rituals to prepare for the tasks (i.e., sharpening pencils, straightening out papers, socializing with others, going to the bathroom) before beginning the task at hand. Yet methods to prepare for tasks that differ from those of the teacher provide further opportunities for misinterpretation. Teachers may mistakenly interpret those behaviors as signs of avoidance and assume that students are being noncompliant when they do not respond immediately to "directives."[4]

For some African-American students, schools are viewed as antagonistic controlling environments. When school codes appear meaningless and controlling, such students may become confrontational. A spiraling effect sometimes occurs when teachers expect students to engage in behaviors that they perceive as meaningless and controlling; the students become combative and further violate the schools' norms, and the teacher feels justified in referring the student for discipline that excludes

---

[4] Townsend

them from that very setting. As more African-American students are suspended than any other group (Skiba et al., 1997), negative attitudes about their ability to abide by school norms are perpetuated.[5]

Real Life example:

    A Math teacher punishes a student with a referral out of the classroom for being "disruptive." The student laughed when another student offered a private joke, and after the teacher announced "You couldn't have been paying attention to the lesson since there is nothing funny about math," the student was excused from the classroom. In this particular school, small infractions are additive; that is to say, after a certain number of "referrals" out of class (which also result in "detention" for the same infractions), a suspension can be assigned. Students can be forced to be absent from classroom learning after say, one laughing incident, one talking in class episode, maybe incomplete homework or not in uniform. The double and often triple-tiered punishment of referral and detention, coupled with the threat of future suspension for the same action (for which the student has already been disciplined) can lead to feelings of perceived unfair attacks by the school and feelings of powerlessness over one's ability to adequately serve one's "sentence" for any given "crime."

    Here lies another example of what could be described as psychological violence. The arbitrary, unpredictable and inconsistent nature with which punishments are received by African-American males can lead to feelings of harassment and intimidation. This climate and the patterns perpetrated

---

[5] Townsend

by the power imbalance over time can lead to student anxiety, depression or disengagement.

Brenda Townsend goes on to chronicle that the communication style of African-American students (both verbal and non-verbal), their preference for maintaining relationships within the classroom, and their unique learning styles can make cultural misinterpretation a precursor to perceived behavioral issues and the resultant disparate discipline that often follows.

In her article "The Impact of Zero Tolerance School Discipline Policies: Issues of Exclusionary Discipline," written while a doctoral student in the Urban Education/School Psychology program at the University of Wisconsin-Milwaukee, Amy Nelson attributes high rates of school suspension and expulsion rates to racism and bias, specifically institutional racism. School policies are often designed by individuals raised with White middle-class values and the assumption is made that all students are raised with a similar perspective. [6] In their research, Fenning and Rose, both of Loyola University Chicago, discovered that minority students were more likely to be suspended for nonviolent issues, such as class disruption and disrespecting teacher authority. Thus, these students are more likely to be punished because of the teacher's lack of behavior management, lack of connection with the teacher or school, or unclear classroom rules.

Yet, when punishing students, schools fail to examine whether student disrespect could be the result of school factors as well. Delpit (1995) also believes that cultural differences between students and teachers cause increases in referrals, including discipline and special education, because of biases held by teachers. Delpit argues that schools are often structured from a White middle-class perspective and if teachers are not direct and clear in their

---

[6] Nelson

expectations, students who do not come from a White or middle-class background are at a disadvantage. Students who are less knowledgeable of the rules are then more likely to be referred to the office and receive punishment, when in reality it was a result of cultural miscommunication.[7]

Real Life Example:

Two African-American male students are asked to leave the classroom for talking. They comply and sit outside the classroom with no further instruction given. The teacher returns after a long recess and asks the students to return to the class. One student whispers to the other, "Wow, if she put us out for that, I wonder what would happen if we really did something bad." The other student whispered his reply, "We would probably get suspended." The teacher, thinking she heard the second student say, "This is bullshit," promptly turned to the student and shouted for him to leave the classroom and go to the office. The student, obviously confused, tried to plead his case. When it was clear that this was unsuccessful, the student decided the best course of action to be to get his backpack and personal things and go to the office. The teacher announced that he could not get his things and must report straight to the office. The standoff continued until the student decided to retrieve his personal belongings despite her protests. He was ultimately suspended for acting "aggressively" toward the teacher. When the student, teacher and parent conference was held and the teacher and administrators realized the misunderstanding, the student was suspended anyway for inappropriate "aggressive" behavior. The teacher's clear lack of respect and control in the situation went unrecognized and worse, was not rectified.

---

[7] Nelson

The "School to Prison Pipeline" has been described and validated by many. The phenomenon not only traces the plight of students who are marginalized and pushed out of the educational system, but also draws attention to similarities between the two systems. Schools have become pre-detention centers for many students; conditioning and preparing them for a life of ultimate confinement. Consider the following similarities between many urban educational centers with predominant African-American populations and government correctional facilities.

	School	Prison
Uniforms	Often compulsory- when required can be grounds for discipline if not worn	Compulsory
Additive discipline, probation and permanent behavior record	Escalating discipline can be based on same infraction. No "new slate" philosophy	Probation violations grounds for repeat incarceration, "Three strikes" laws
Pyramid admin/ discipline structure	Principal, Counselors, Teachers	Warden, Deputies, Prison guards

	School	Prison
Compulsory participation	Truancy considered criminal	Full captivity
Control of movement with sensory conditioning	Loud bells announce permission to move about campus	Alarms, bells, buzzers signal movement between areas
Locked campus with security force controlling entry and exit	Many are gated and locked, some with metal detectors. Security guards as gate keepers	Gated Guards as gate keepers
Absolute social control	Dominant culture determines if and when one is a suitable citizen	Dominant culture determines if and when one is a suitable citizen

There are also similarities that can be drawn between the school policies of detention and prison-readiness.

	Detention	Prison
Revocation of Freedom	No freedom of movement, speech or actions	No freedom of movement, speech or actions
May be linked to compulsory labor	May include compulsory school clean up	often evidence for "good behavior" and can lessen sentence.
Biased sentencing	African Americans over-represented	African Americans over-represented
Additive	Prior sentencing can be used to determine future sentencing	Prior sentencing can be used to determine future sentencing
Evidence of benefit to individual or society	Lacking	Lacking

The clash of the cultures many African-American students face when entering and enduring the Euro-American Educational system can have profound and lasting consequences. The clash of the psyches, the systematic fragmenting of the African personality, the miscommunication of knowledge and the misinterpretation of behavior, the devaluation of the African worldview and the criminalization of the African principle in the Euro-American educational system all combine to create an explosion of such proportions, that the African-American student can be dismembered, disemboweled and violently overcome in the process.

The education of African-American children is complex, given the opposing nature of the two cultures they find themselves in. The solution can seem elusive. However, it is clear that many of the philosophical, cultural and communication barriers that currently exist within the educational arena can be mitigated by the African-American community reclaiming the education of our youth. Only by doing this will we re-enforce those values and amplify those abilities inherent in our young people. Safe spaces will be created for them to embrace and unleash their African personality. In the process, we may even close the gate that leads multitudes of our young men from the path of self-awareness to the prison pipeline.

Community in Healing and Educating

The intention of creating this book was manyfold. I seek to explain the experience of my children and others within the current educational model. I seek to examine the likely roots and origins of the challenges faced within that system for our children. I seek to hint at ways we, the "whole" parents of these "whole" children can shield them from systematic fragmentation and victimization and arm them against psychological warfare. In the following pages you will find a series of interviews of ordinary African-American community members. They speak not only from some external marker of expertise (as many are experts in their respective fields), but also as those who have successfully taught and are teaching African-American children from a place of wholeness: from a place of living, breathing, moving knowledge: and from an unseen and powerful place.

The first interview is with Allen Scott Gordon, an African-American science and math teacher in Oakland, California. He has a background in journalism and was a student of public schools himself. He teaches African-American male youth daily and has a very unique perspective on the needs of his students, along with a keen awareness of the challenges that accompany his task as a teacher.

JayVon Muhammad is a midwife and entrepreneur. She discusses the choices she and her husband have made regarding the education of their children. The decisions we make to take control of our young people's education are captured in this family's attempt to ensure they groom a group of children grounded in self-confidence.

In our interview with Kelly Clark, we find that the issue of competent teaching rises to the top of a good education. Kelly Clark teaches elementary students in the San Francisco school district and finds that no matter the color of the students, a teacher must be organized and prepared on a daily basis to meet the challenges of teaching an increasingly diversified student body. Her observations are both insightful and valuable.

The interviews included in this work, both individual and group, are purposeful. My perspective in writing about the tragedy of the education of African-American youth, specifically our young men is that of a mother, healer, teacher and community member. But just as the African worldview is whole, so is our collective experience. The perspectives of the men and women I have included in this work, are like a call and response. It's my "Amen." They are witness to the undoing. They are the high fives after a well-fought battle, cheers from team members. They are the silent nods from knowing elders and ancestors. They are me. We are each other. One must be at peace to heal, not in pieces, and we know that words have power. So here we go.

IV. THE INNER CIRCLE-MICROCOSM

Interview with Allen Scott Gordon
African-American
high school teacher in Oakland public school district
Oakland, California

Can you give me some background information about yourself? Where did you attend high school and college and where did you receive your teaching credentials?

ASG: I am a native Californian and graduated from Oakland High School in 1989. I graduated from Grambling State University with a degree in Mass Communications and Journalism. Though I had aspirations to teach school, my journalism aspirations were much stronger and I pursued that path in 1992 when I completed my first internship at, *The Source* magazine, the leading youth culture periodical at the time. My journey into the field of education began when I returned to Oakland in 2004 and applied for a substitute teaching credential with Oakland Public Schools in 2005.

I know you went to an HBCU. Were there many other brothers going into teaching? What were some of the reasons given for and against entering the teaching profession? What was the conversation around education for our youth?

ASG: Most of the students in the Education field at Grambling were overwhelmingly women. Very few men. Many of the women in the education field were from families where their parents were educators and saw this as a noble profession to continue. Most of the males I know who went into to teaching actually were students who majored in History, economics, criminal law, and mathematics. We all belonged to a study group called the Sons and Daughters of Imhotep and our main focus was studying about our ancestors from Africa and around the diaspora and creating ways to improve and empower our communities. We all ended up teaching school at various levels, but only three males ended up being education majors. All of these men were pretty clear on what their visions were concerning Black youth in education. It was a daily discussion and passion.

What subject(s) do you teach? How long have you been teaching and in what settings (i.e. public or private schools, urban or suburban setting)?

ASG: The subject I am pursuing my credential in is single-subject math for secondary education. By looking at my background, I should be teaching an English class or Social Science, but my first assignment (2005-2006 school year) as a substitute teacher was filling a vacancy in algebra at Ralph J. Bunche Academy in Oakland. RJBA is a public continuation high school and was considered pretty rough because of the type of kids that were enrolled. I could explain and instruct Algebra with relative ease. I was given five math classes with the majority of kids who were too much for the other two math teachers to handle. Many of [the students] were below their grade level, but I didn't have any problems and the kids were engaged in the process and started to excel. I was at RJBA for three of the seven years I have been teaching. I've also had long and short-term assignments at other schools teaching a variety of subjects to elementary, middle and high schools. I think that, as an individual pursuing teaching after having a previous profession outside of education, I needed to do as much on all levels as a substitute to see what grade level and subject would best suit me in pursuing a full-time teaching credential and Masters degree or to abandon the notion all together.

I've taught Biology and Physical Science at the high school level and English of course. But Social Science and Algebra/Geometry were the subjects I was strongest in and where student improvement was greatest.

Tell me about your other interests? You do some writing, correct? What about your experience in the entertainment industry? How do you think it altered your approach to teaching?

ASG: I am a journalist and writer by profession and passion. This I have been doing for 20 years in various publications (*The Source, Rap Pages, Vibe*), daily newspapers, documentary films, advertising copy, music anthologies, as well as working on my own book. My travels and experience have been of great influence on how I relate to young Black males in the classroom. It can be encouraging to some or a reaffirmation to others who dream or plan to do or see something different in their life pursuits.

You probably also know that the number of African-American male teachers are decreasing and some think that is one reason why AA males don't do as well since there are fewer role models in education. What made you choose teaching as a profession? Why don't you think more African-American men choose teaching as a profession?

ASG: I chose to teach early on in college, but was swept into the glamour of the entertainment industry after doing my first internship in 1992 at *The Source*. I [then] needed to do something different and I thought education might be the field where my talents were most effective at home. All of the "save the community Black power talk" I had to now put into real action. Teaching is a very noble profession. I didn't have as much as an appreciation for it in college as I do now because it wasn't sexy. Lawyers, doctors, federal law enforcement, entertainment professions, media anchors, international business, all that stuff is sexy - high paying salaries, luxury cars and homes- so-called status symbols of success, at least from what we see in media, film and television. And to say that Americans are not influenced by the media is to ignore how powerful media is in shaping opinions and lifestyles. We learned in journalism school that "The media doesn't tell you what to think, just what to think about." All of the sexy shows on TV or major film dramas involve people in professions other than teaching. "Wall Street," "Law & Order," "CSI," "24," "The Cosby Show," etc. Money and lifestyle are constantly promoted, not shows about teachers or where school is the primary setting for a show. The lone exceptions are comedies like "Glee," which has little to do with education, or the fourth season of "The Wire," which should be aired weekly and shown in schools and teachers' training.

Where do you teach now? Do you teach African-American youth where you work? What percentage of your classes are specifically AA males?

ASG: In March of 2012, I filled in a long-term vacancy at my alma mater, Oakland High School. My classes are 60 percent African-American, and about 30 percent of that population are African-American males.

Are there any particular surprises you've encountered teaching this group of students? Did it match your expectations?

ASG: I haven't had any surprises among the students academically. The males typically grasp mathematical concepts and solving equations without much difficulty. The challenge lies in motivation to succeed or complete tasks with regularity (homework), standardized test taking, attention span, and vocabulary, which is the challenge in all other subjects. Kids don't do much reading or watching shows that challenge their thinking (A&E, PBS, Discovery), and their vocabulary is limited, which affects their comprehension of biology, social studies, chemistry, language arts, English, and of course foreign languages. Then there is the issue of electronic wireless devices and access to the internet. That is a constant distraction for kids in and outside of the classroom.

Do you think your influence on the students is different than that of your non-African-American colleagues? If so, in what way?

ASG: Yes, I think I have a certain amount of influence being an African-American male, especially being from Oakland. I think the rapport I have works in that the students have a voice with me. I'm not judgmental, but I'm stern and truthful. Very consistent and never wavering on principle. I think that is a quality along with caring and sincerity that is appreciated or tolerated by the students. For the most part, some of my colleagues over the years just perform the duties of their teaching job, such as delivering the lesson and nothing more. They are very mechanical in the relationship with students. But "I say, you do" doesn't really foster or inspire greatness or the desire to grow and prosper. Just to complete a task when told? As you know, kids will buck authority when it seems unfair, unruly, or weak.

What are your thoughts about how we can turn around how our youth think about school and perform once they get there? What have you noticed works? What doesn't work?

ASG: Complete overhaul is the only solution. From the school system and curriculum to the teachers and administrators, and of course the parents and how they foster learning in their children from elementary to high school. Parents as a whole should be outraged, but they aren't and therefore the changes that happen in the education system are not dictated by parents, but by politicians and academicians who have little to no clue about how to turn this ship around. There's a lot of intellectual masturbation that produces nothing. What does work? Two parent households or strong single parenthood that focuses on the needs of children, family and community. That may sound like a platitude, but the proof is empirical. Stability fosters stability, be it emotional, educational, etc.

Interview with JayVon Muhammad
Married mother of three children with two grandchildren. Licensed midwife, writer, successful entrepreneur Muslim in the Nation of Islam for over 15 years.

> "Our children should be trained in our own schools, not dropped into the schools of the enemy where they are taught that whites have been and will be world rulers."
> -*Message to the Black Man in America*

Tell me some reasons you chose to send your children to Muhammad University for their education.

JM: Schools throughout the Nation of Islam are named Muhammad University of Islam (MUI). The education that students receive at MUI is relevant and excellent. Students learn all the core subjects taught in public school with an emphasis on science and math. They also learn the truth about *their* history, *their* nature, and God. History is taught in a way where the students can see themselves and their people in it. I have witnessed a positive transformation in many children from the community while attending MUI.

Would you say that other members of the African-American community feel or felt the same way you do?

JM: When Muhammad University of Islam opened in San Francisco, it didn't take long before families from the community were knocking on the doors asking if their children could attend. Next thing we knew, there were many families from the community that were not members of the Nation of Islam, sending their children to our schools.

What would you say was the biggest, most compelling thing that separated MUI education from that of the public school system?

JM: In public schools today, God is a forbidden subject. Prayer is not allowed, and the mention of God is discouraged, as God's name could be considered offensive to some. Culturally, God has always been a part of our lives, be it education, marriage, trials, joys and in some way we include God in our decisions.

One of the larger reasons that we chose to send our children to Muhammad University of Islam was that the education was centered on God. A typical day at Muhammad University of Islam begins with prayer. Prayer is followed by the Pledge, and the pledge is followed by a song. Children then repeat an inspirational mantra before being dismissed to their classes. The inspirational mantra includes things like, I love myself, I love my parents, I love my community, I have a responsibility. It is a beautiful thing.

You have often fondly mentioned how structured the environment is. Can you offer some examples?

JM: Muhammad University of Islam provides a very structured environment. Modest, neat, and clean uniforms are worn by all students. Boys and girls are taught in separate classrooms, and have little to no contact with one another throughout the day.

When at all possible, men teach boys and women teach girls. This is a practice that my husband and I thought very important. We wanted to ensure that our son would be able to admire and respect his teacher, and also receive justice in the classroom.

Our daughter also benefited from being taught by a godly black woman. She was able to witness appropriate mannerism, speech, femininity, behavior, etc. In our society today, we often don't deem it important for girls to learn proper etiquette and how to behave like ladies. It is very important, and we appreciated this opportunity afforded to our daughter.

There are some credentialed teachers, and some aren't. The beautiful thing is that all the teachers there are qualified, interested, willing, and committed. They have a sincere interest in making our children better. They are not there simply for a paycheck.

It's interesting you mention that. Many women I speak to point to that sincerity as being critical to their children's success.

JM: Yes, another driving factor of our decision to enroll our children in MUI was the love factor. Let's face it; love is something that our children don't get at public school. In fact, in many cases our children get the opposite of love. Muhammad University of Islam is a love-filled environment. Students are greeted at the door by a smiling face, and sometimes a hug. When I dropped my children off there was a sense of relief. I didn't have to worry about racism, of teachers injuring my children's self-esteem. It was just an environment of love and trust.

Kind of an extension of the home?

JM: Yes. Foundational components of Muhammad University of Islam are discipline, respect and integrity. Muhammad University of Islam does not tolerate lying, cheating, stealing, offensive language or behavior, disrespect, violence, etc. All of these behaviors are addressed in the manner most effective by the appropriate and designated staff.

More rigorous than a home environment might be, but still with the underlying love, trust and sincerity. Tell me about the nutritional program offered.

JM: Students are not allowed to bring a lunch into the school, but rather a home-cooked style lunch is prepared at the school and served to students every day. The practice of cooking lunch on-site was instituted after the realization that many parents did not send their children with nutritional lunches, and some were sent with no lunch at all. The lunches prepared at MUI are nutritionally balanced, and prevent children from being bombarded and overwhelmed by non-nutritious lunches, sugar and junk food. Lunch is included in the affordable tuition charged by the school.

That brings me to the question of cost. Many of our folk find private schools out of their reach financially. Tell me about the tuition at MUI.

JM: Because Muhammad University of Islam is a private school, there is a fee (tuition). The tuition is affordable. There is some flexibility for those with multiple children, and a sliding fee scale for families who cannot afford the regular tuition. The Administration strives to ensure that all families who desire to send their children to MUI have the opportunity.

Are their any final thoughts you would like to share?

JM: As Black parents we can no longer afford to offer our children to our Open Enemy. You might ask why I say Open Enemy. Well, in the years that education has been desegregated what have our children learned? What is their condition? We are serving up our children's very mind.

If we are going to be active players in this world, we have to teach our own. We have to teach our children the knowledge that our Enemy refuses to.

I would recommend Muhammad University of Islam to our entire community. We have all suffered in the United States under today's educational system, but like with all other social ills, none have suffered quite like the Black Man and Black Woman. Time to make a change!

Interview with Kelly Clark
African-American 5th grade teacher
Harvey Milk Elementary School
2014 Teacher of the Year
San Francisco, California
(Interviewed by Ajuana Black)

In regards to the African-American boys you have worked with at Harvey Milk, what thoughts come to you?

KC: That's a really broad question because kids come from different communities.

Well, does education look different in some communities compared to others?

KC: Well there [can be] an imbalance of power where the parents are not empowered. So they don't know how to access what they need. You [can] have different values that are interfacing with no webs of connection, other than the human capacity and what's mandated. [Teachers] have to look beyond what is mandated and look at what people need. Anytime you mandate something, there's going to be a disconnect . There's this invisible hand that enforces things without even knowing the specific needs of the people that you're trying to service.

Is more challenging to deliver the education to children who are low-income?

KC: It depends on who's standing in front of them. All the kids that come from communities that are dealing with societal injustices are not coming the same way. Just because you have the same zip code doesn't mean you have certain behaviors. That's an assumption. You just have to be mindful not to pigeonhole people based on having a poor appearance or having a single mom who didn't graduate from high school. It doesn't mean you don't come to school ready to learn.

How have you dealt with different types of children coming from different types of backgrounds?

KC: My approach is that I'm well rested. My approach is to deal with myself. That I'm really well prepared. That my lessons are planned. They are written. I am not confused about my purpose. So I don't confuse them about their purpose. So it starts with me. I mean I'm happy. I'm happy to see them. I come in open-hearted. That's first and foremost: I show up right. If you are dealing with children in a certain age group...like boys almost at any age group just have a lot of energy.
My expectations are ridiculous and I tell them that. But I also say, "You can do it." And then I help them. When they do it and they smile, I give them a pat on the back. You give them some hugs. You give them some love. You come completely nurturing. If you are going to push really hard, you must be nurturing. But this is for anybody. If you want to make the world better, you don't make it better for one group of people, you make it better for all the people. If one kid needs it, all the kids need it. It's not like there's this one little Black boy and he lives over here and he needs it. Actually, if he needs it, you have to be crazy not to think all the children don't need it. And if you only teach a certain way to a certain group of people, then how can you create change for everybody if you
don't teach to everybody?

I can see teaching to the whole group. On the other hand, it's like saying everybody is the same. But everyone isn't the same. Sometimes children

do call for something different.

KC: Since I have a diverse class and I am in there by myself with them, here's what I know for sure: I don't think there is a certain way to teach certain children. I think you have to come really well prepared and really flexible. Instead of being a tree trunk, you have to be a bamboo. Teacher Education programs are not set up to teach you how to teach to everyone. It's kind of like Gap, "We'll make a 36/28 and everybody better be able to fit it. Well, actually most people aren't that size. So if you are going to teach a wide range of children, you have to read everything.
Your professional development must be in order. You have to understand community. I put it back on the teacher. The teacher is where the river hits the road. What kind of special stuff does the kid need? What? They need some cereal? They need to get up and wiggle around? That's not just specific to poor, Black children. They don't need "special stuff." The teacher is the one that needs "special stuff."

Your're right. I would put it back on the teacher.

KC: If you see a kid coming to school, you have to have the wherewithal to say, what did you eat for breakfast? And then wait for them to answer. You have to be patient. If you know you have a kid that is not at grade level at reading, then you have to shelter the lesson. "We're just going to do it the special way for every kid that comes into the class that looks like you?" Come on now. That's not fair. I'm going to put you in a literacy group. Instead of putting you in a homogenous literacy group where everybody is reading the same, I'm going to put you in a literacy group where other kids can support you.

I have heard teachers say the Black kids in my class act like "this" and I am having a hard time connecting with them.

kKC: Well I would like to challenge them and say, what did your evening look like before you went in there? What did you do? How much did you know you were going to do? What does your lesson look like? What were you specifically targeting? What was your goal for the day?

When the teacher is present with and prepared for the students they have in the class, no matter where those children come from, no matter what background, there still should be some type of way where everyone gets taught in a very respectful and honorable way.

KC: Yes. I think it's really complicated and most folks, self included; when you go into the classroom your tool kit is not full. You do not have all the tools you need. You got a plier, a screwdriver...

...and then you get this one student that's like needing something completely different than what you have.

KC: And usually it's not a whole bunch of kids. It's usually one kid that throws things off. So you better have prepared a lesson for that one kid. The thing is that all kids come different and we focus so heavenly on the Black kids as you say. If you think there is just one variable to teaching, you're wrong. We'll just change this, then it will be fixed. You have to connect with the family. Be honest with the family. Go see who those kids are.

I had all these parents make parent conferences with me and they didn't even show up. Yes I'm irritated, but bottom line is I'm still going to meet that kid's needs. As long as I'm going to be in the public school, I gotta be willing to do what it takes. It's going to be back-breaking, grinding kind of stuff. In order to do a good job, you have to really work hard.

Last question. Why do you not agree with home schooling?

KC: I am not a fan of homeschooling. I'm not a fan of it because we highlight those times when it's successful and we act like it's the end all to be all.

What about home schooling do you think doesn't work?

I don't think that it doesn't work. I think it works for some people. Basically humans are social. Sometimes people are trying to opt out of the inevitable. I would rather have a nine month-old learning how to walk than a nine year-old learning how to walk. The skills that you need to get along in society are broad. They are diverse. Get them in there and support them. Don't isolate them. Some kids? Yes.

I only have six right now at my homeschool and it's incredibly social. I do think that is one of the myths about homeschooling. That they don't get a lot of social skills.

KC: I think you are doing a different type of homeschooling. One, it's not just your children. Most people just homeschool their own families. Secondly, I'm not looking at this through one, little, single lens. I recognize it's broad and a lot of different things going on. I'm not saying that kids can't be social with a few other kids. I get that it works okay for some kids. I'm just a fan of a whole bunch of people. I love watching little kindergartners learn how to jump rope. I love watching them play four square. I was just talking with a first-grader on Friday night; we went star gazing. He said, "Oh no, I don't play four square." I said, "Why don't you play four square?" He said, " The older kids do that." This six year old was explaining to me why he plays handball as oppose to four square. And I wasn't trying to say, "but...but ...but.." I was just listening. That's what I'm talking about. Where he could say, "there are all of these kids..." I was just happy to hear him have a broad experience about it. That's what I'm looking at. I'm not saying homeschool doesn't work for anybody. If I had children, I wouldn't choose it for them. I would choose a lot of things for kids. I would put them all in there. They'll be alright.

Reflections from One Home School Teacher
Ajuana Black
Founder & Head Teacher of
Beams Village Academy, West Oakland, CA

The New York Times reported in March 2012 that, "Although Black students made up only 18 percent of those enrolled in the schools sampled, they accounted for 35 percent of those suspended once, 46 percent of those suspended more than once and 39 percent of all expulsions, according to the Civil Rights Data Collection's 2009-10 statistics from 72,000 schools in 7,000 districts, serving about 85 percent of the nation's students."

As an educator who has taught within the charter, public, private, independent, and most recently for the last six years, homeschool setting, it is very clear to me that something is amiss with the process of educating African-American males. It is my personal belief that if culture is not present within the classroom consistently, reflecting and affirming the child that is being taught, the education that is being administered is somewhat faulty. It is not sufficient.

I believe that education must be holistic. Within the process of education there are cultural, historical, & emotional connections that must be made regarding the child who is being taught, or the education is not effective. I also firmly believe that how a teacher views a child is a direct determination to how effective the teacher will be in their approach. My question is how much are educators connecting culturally with African-American youth? To what degree are non-African-American educators demonstrating an unconditional respect and honoring the African-American students who walk into their classrooms? If you are flooded with subliminal as well as blatant, low-standard images and messages of young African-American males in society that tell you they are broken and disadvantage, how can the education that is given by these teachers be effective? The perceptions that teachers carry with them, whether they are aware of them or not, are a contributing factor to their lack of effectiveness in connecting with African-American male students. There is more to teaching and receiving a thorough and quality education than teaching concepts, theories and academic processes.

Looking back at African-American educators and the schools that existed during the era of pre-emancipation within the United States, there is overwhelming evidence of the importance of connecting with students not only on an academic level, but on an emotional, cultural and historical level as well. Let's take a look back at what African-American teachers were doing in the pre-emancipation era, a period where it was evident that African- American people were going through a very tragic existence within America.

African-American educators were very clear about their own community's existence and what the goal was: to obtain a thorough education that would be the vehicle to take them to the next level of true liberation. This country was not in support of this goal. We were living in a society that did not support the education of African-American people and the educators of that time knew this fact. However they were extremely driven and determined to not only be educated, but to build institutions that would holistically drive the machine that would educate our communities at large. The ongoing legacy of this commitment to self-education in the African-American community is evident in the more than 100 African-American colleges and universities still thriving in the United States today. The educators of our community were clearly aware that this society did not view African-Americans as human, much less human beings with the capacity to learn. Therefore, what sense would it make to turn to them and request their aid in teaching our own?

In the book entitled *A Class Their Own*, Joseph C. Price, an African-American teacher, made extremely clear the importance of African- American teachers teaching African-American students by stating, "The future educators of the Blacks both in America and Africa, are the Blacks." (Joseph C. Price, diary entry, 1877). These African-American educators were completely connected with these students historically. Not only were they connected with the education of the younger ones of the community, but they had a vested interest in the whole race being educated. Elijah P. Marrs, one of Kentucky's first Black teachers stated in *A Class of Their Own,* "I was convinced that there could be something for me to do in the future that I could not accomplish by remaining in ignorance." There was such a diligence for learning and raising the literacy rate within the Black community, *A Class of Their Own* states, that "by 1865 at least 400,000 people possessed some degree of literacy."

A Class of Their Own goes on to explain that [the development of] private schools represented a creative response to Black ambition when the public schools ranged from bad to nonexistent. This completely reflects our current state today. Private schools also sowed the seeds of class inequality. In charging tuition (fees), they gave an advantage to Black families who could afford to pay for schooling. Most Black families could not or would not. Moreover, educational advantage translated into economic advantage. In dispensing an education that was usually better than that provided by the public schools, private schools widened the distance between the two groups." (pg. 220) Private schools would never reach more than a small minority of Black children. In order to end mass illiteracy and improve education for the vast majority, there had to be more and better public schools. Such improvements would depend, overwhelmingly, upon Black women.

There was a complete purpose to become literate and to pursue an education and the community understood they would all benefit from this goal. I believe they wanted to see each other succeed. If your fellow man or woman was literate, in the Black community's eyes, that meant the community as a whole moved that much closer to societal mobility. Basically, they were in it to win it together! Behind the education was an intention that validated the African-American student.

The Government Doesn't Know

There is this thought that the government thinks about everyone equally and pursues everyone's best interests. If African-American people did not start off in this country being the "apple of this country's eye," when did that change? With the diversification of the United States population and the ongoing efforts to fight racial injustices, perceptions of what constitutes an adequate education are evolving. However, it's evident that most public schools have a challenging time servicing so many different types of cultures and backgrounds.

When public schools started, they did not know how to be inclusive and deal with diversity. Sadly, even now they don't. Our government continues to struggle with this dilemma. It expresses willingness to engage all cultures and has the highest educational intentions for all children represented in the school system. In reality, the government policies around education often alienate those same cultures that they are attempting to engage. Furthermore, if the dominant European culture that created the atrocities which occurred on our people has never formally acknowledged their role in the under-education of African people, how could we even begin to think that their efforts toward a better education now is sincere and inclusive of our African-American young men?

We should not look to the government to make sure our children are receiving the best education. We need to look to ourselves as a community to provide a higher standard of education and remain advocates for our children's future.

Just Not Interested

Post-slavery, the government was not interested in black upward mobility at all. It was not interested in Blacks becoming educated to a high level. This being the case, resources were extremely low for our schools. Has this changed? NO. The whole melting pot theory that all cultures can exist in America and receive the same type of education is a farce because the government is not interested or invested in everyone equally. We must make sure our young males are getting the nourishment they need at the educational table. It is my belief that this current educational environment does not demonstrate a vigilant interest in getting our boys educated.

A Class Their Own describes that even during the post-reconstruction era, the White public schools had a lack of resources and therefore even less energy was dedicated to African-American Schools. "Freedman Bureau reached 10% of the Black school population. Because of Reconstruction, every state had established a system of public schools." You would think this fact would be beneficial to our people. It goes on to state, "But the ability of that fledgling system to enroll more Black children depended upon Black initiation." (p101) The fact that the initiation by the Black community be present in order for the enrollment to go up within the public schools shows the direct correlation of the importance of the power of the community. The result was a cohesiveness that was developed amongst the community. It's as if they were on a mission together. Education, community and businesses development were interconnected thru the process of African-Americans creating their own education system. As a result, the community continued to self-educate with a sense of urgency. They could see how it directly affected their future.

Our Vision Has Shifted

Our educational vision has now shifted from one of self-reliance to one of reliance on the government. We seem to have abandoned our own responsibilities on the ground level. Collectively, like our ancestors did when there was nowhere for them to look, we must turn and look to ourselves for our own answers. We must decide and see what our own vision is for ourselves. I believe our vision has become murky due to integration and the belief that we are suppose to embrace society's vision of, or lack of, real education.

When Academics Ignores Culture
How Culture and Education Form Beliefs of Adequacy or Inadequacy

I grew up in a home where my mother, an African-American, valued education to an extremely high degree. She was born in 1924, a time period where our community valued education very seriously. She demonstrated her commitment to the "best education" by putting me in a traditional Irish Catholic school taught by Irish nuns with a population of predominantly Italian & Chinese children. Out of 500 students, there were 10 black children. I was one of the ten. I commuted from a predominately Black and Latino neighborhood in East Oakland, California and traveled on three buses to get to San Francisco to my school, St. Brigid's, in San Francisco everyday. From kindergarten to the eighth grade, I had only White teachers. That felt like the norm for me. In this school, my culture did not matter nor was it really acknowledged. There wasn't even a token "Black History" celebration or report given in class. When I got my hair corn-rowed, they told my mother I couldn't wear the beads. Attending St. Brigid's was all about the very standard Euro-centric education, Catholicism, and belief in a religious God.

The defining moment for me, when I told myself and truly believed I could not understand science, was in the third grade. I was in science class with my fellow Chinese and Italian classmates. We were involved in a science experiment that had us using test tubes. When it came time to pour the solutions in the different tubes, I became confused and asked a simple question on which solutions went in which tubes. Ms. Wolf abruptly had me stand up directly from my seat and loudly answered, "You don't even know that!" All 20 some-odd students looked at me in complete silence. I continued to look at Ms. Wolf as if searching for the answer in her head. But after she instructed me to sit down, I made an absolute decision in my mind that I did not understand science, I could not understand science, and I would not ever understand it.

In addition to the invalidating White educational environment I was experiencing on a daily basis, my cultural home roots had nothing there to confirm the concept and study of science. Of course, now that I am older and an educator, I recognize that science is all throughout our normal existence. However, as a young eight year-old African-American girl growing up in East Oakland, California, I could not see how science was relevant to me. Science seemed like a foreign language and I could not see or find any examples in my real life. It appeared to be so different from my home life. There was nothing in my home that looked like the test tubes in my classroom. The vocabulary used in the classroom did not connect to any words I used at home with my family. Therefore, there became an enormous disconnect between the world of science and myself. Furthermore, an unfortunate belief took root in that non-affirming educational environment that I could not understand science. I started to think that something was wrong with me, so much so, that science was incomprehensible.

Many students today experience the same daunting reality. What they are being taught in class more and more feels so foreign to their "real" world that they develop the belief that they can't comprehend, that school is not for them, and then they proceed to check out of pursuing their education to completion.

When Academics Meets Culture

An excellent example of science being made relevant to an African-American community is the overall experience that was created at ASA Academy & Community Science Center. ASA Academy and Community Science Center was founded and directed by Tovi Scruggs and Sharon Parker. It was an African-American private middle and high school that also had a community science center. Both Tovi and Sharon had been public school teachers who, after noticing that system fail African-American students, decided to open a private African-American school. Their vision and pedagogy made sure that all content studied and instructed was relevant to the African-American culture. The students not only learned about a multitude of Black scientists in history, but Mrs. Parker made sure the students researched current African-American scientists and the specific fields they were focused on.

Many of the teachers who were teaching science were of color if not African-American. Just as in many schools where Einstein is the example for brilliance, the school's computer lab (one of many) was named after Philip Emeagwali, a Nigerian who was instrumental in establishing the Internet. The science center also produced monthly science workshops for the community, which clearly made science much more relevant to the students of the school and the immediate community. Often science focused on projects and issues that directly affected the community. One relevant hands-on science project was the asthma investigation. The science center had the students research the reasons the asthma rate was so high in West Oakland, which was the community that several of the ASA students resided in.

Another wonderful example of academics meeting culture was with West Oakland Community School (WOCS), a charter middle school that focused on educating and servicing mostly African-American children. This school showed an incredible demonstration of honoring the child and his/her background. It used the ancient African philosophy of the MAAT principles as part of the school foundation. They also valued the students by speaking to where the child came from on a cultural level. In addition, all of the teachers were African-American and had a good sense of the history and experience of African-American people. Therefore, the teachers brought this awareness and understanding with them when they taught.

I had the privilege of teaching at both of these schools. I witnessed a village being created around these children. This village reflected and confirmed their worth to them everyday. The teachers honored and respected these children and were willing to take the time to develop a curriculum that validated and honored their own culture. As a result of this culturally based, affirming education, the African-American students demonstrated a high sense of self-worth, a strong work ethic and a commitment to community. The students were able to witness how education affects the integrity of the community and vice-versa. Both ASA and WOCS nurtured an environment where African-American students saw members of their own community as teachers, administrators, scientists, community leaders and self-governed businessmen and women. This reflection allowed them to see those possibilities in themselves.

V. THE CENTER-AFRICAN CHILDREN'S MANIFESTO

How to Be a Parent Champion™: Doing Your Part to Close the Achievement Gap
By Tovi Scruggs, M.Ed.

This segment of *African Children's Manifesto* offers guidance and expert advice to parents who are looking for and are in need of additional support to create both school success and a college-going attitude outside of school. This chapter will coach you into a Parent Champion™- parents who are able to successfully champion the academic success of their children. The Parent Champion™ is being shared as an empowerment model of support that can be implemented immediately to increase parent engagement and student success.

This portion of Manifesto will:
- Inspire you to be better partners with teachers and the school;
- Empower you with tools to support your child's academic success;
- Educate you on how to create a "college-going" attitude at home; and
- Create peace in your home from a shared set of expectations about school

Parent Champions™ are committed to winning school success and academic achievement for their children. Parent Champions demonstrate this commitment with appropriate actions and choices regarding their child's education. When school succeeds, true education and college-going become the priority, and the use of time and financial choices are guided by that motivation. Parent Champions focus on what I term "educational parenting", where they are the very best school-partners; they are reflective and take action in regards to how they co-educate, and they partner with their child's school in order to get the best results for their child.

As a parent, YOU are the best champion of your child's success. Period. Being a Parent Champion™ means prioritizing hands-on time and developing strategies for your child and their education. As a parent, when you prioritize time invested in education and educational choices, you are modeling your value for education and, therefore, championing your child's success.

The Critical First Step: Reflecting on Your Parenting

As a parent, you must acknowledge the fact that YOU are your child's first and greatest teacher. Your child begins to learn from you both before and after birth. Your child's success depends on YOU. You must embrace this truth. Once you have a child, you become a parent, it is not an easy job and one not to be taken lightly. As with all jobs that we choose to take on, the job is only done well with focus, investment, and development. The job of "parent" rarely has any other preparation than our own experience as a child, watching others, and then the nine months to strive to earn your Parenting Ph.D. before you get to work with highly intensive on-the-job-training.

As a coach, I value high levels of self-reflection and encourage others to reflect first before beginning any area of personal growth and development. Because you are reading this portion of *African Children's Manifesto*, I trust that you are willing to look at other ways to be a better parent in the area of education – and that is commendable. Reflection and willingness to be better takes courage. As with all areas of personal growth and development, you must be willing to take an honest look at yourself and ask, "Have I been 'parenting' or have I simply been a 'parent'?" As the parent, you are held accountable for actively parenting. As a "parent," you are actively involved in caring for someone else, but "parenting" requires deliberate action from you – a doing to get results. Our greatest accountability lies in how effectively we parent. Yet, we blame the schools while relying on the schools to do what it is that WE should be doing.

What is key in acknowledging your role in educational parenting is this: the school has its job and the home has its job. The school and the home have different jobs, yet they have similar intentions. The "job" of the school is to educate your child as it relates to academic skills. The "job" of the home is to teach, nurture, and support the child as it relates to personal skill sets for success in life. While we may believe and expect that the school's job is more than mere education, it is not realistic in this educational and societal climate as it relates to children of color. Plus, you cannot expect an institution to love your child more than you do. It's up to YOU to do what the school will not. It's YOUR child. Thankfully, the primary intention of the school and home is shared: your child achieves academic success that readies him or her for post-secondary readiness (being prepared for college or the workplace).

Our community has to stop asking the school to do what we know is for us to be doing, for the things that we say that we are to busy to do, the things we do not even know how to do. The school has one primary role: to teach our children the academic skills to prepare them for college. There is nothing else that we can count on them to do for our children, especially when the schools do not reflect what we say we value as a community. It is the job of the parent to partner with the school to get the child to college and to make sure that the child has been taught the various resiliency skills to stay in college and succeed. After it's all said and done: it's your child and you cannot expect anyone to love your child more than you do. They often don't.

There's only one solution: it's not about being right – playing the blame game – it's about doing what's right and what works. What appears normal is not always right. As a parent who is parenting, you must stretch and challenge yourself for the courageous and consuming actions to create a college mind-set and college-going culture in your home. YOU must become the counter-narrative in your child's life because the narrative they get from outside of your home is LOUD. You must always keep in mind that your child spends more waking hours with people other than you. The other people - and the music, the television, the institutions, the programs - they are all communicating a narrative to your child every day. It's a narrative that often must be countered by what you instilled in the beginning, continue to instill, and will instill as you become more re-tooled, re-educated, and empowered.

Since we are reflecting and you are open to Parent Champion™ coaching, I ask you to ask yourself this one hard question – and answer honestly:

"How committed am I to my child's success?"

We invest in what we are committed to. We invest our energy, our time, our talents, our money, and our resources to what we are committed to. As it relates to the success of your child in school, how committed are you to your child's success?

What kind of investment of your energy and time did you make in selecting your child's school? Did you visit first or did you let the enrollment process decide? Did the school's reputation decide? Did word-of-mouth decide? Did convenience decide? How many of you have gone to your child's school - more than to simply enroll, register, drop off the paperwork, and those easy "get him in school" tasks? Some people spend more time investigating and selecting a cell phone to buy than time deciding on their child's school. How much time you spent selecting your child's school is a sign of your level of commitment to your child's success.

    Did you get remedial help for your child if they were performing at a B or lower in a subject? Did you get remedial help for your child if/when you found out they were performing below grade level in reading or math? How immediate and responsive you are to being proactive about academic achievement is a sign of your level of commitment to your child's success.

    Do you know what book your child is reading right now? Our children should be reading books both in and out of school, books that interest and challenge them. The library has thousands of books for free. Not only does that save you money, it's also a wonderful, most memorable, and affordable (free!) way to get quality time with your child. On top of that, YOU sitting with your child while reading a book of your own for 30 minutes each day while your child also reads a book of his own is one of the most impactful examples of the importance of reading that you can provide. I know you know that children (like we all do) look to people's actions more than their words for the truth. Your level of interest in reading and the importance of reading is a sign of your level of commitment to your child's success.

    If it's your biggest dream that your child do well in school and go to college, then ask yourself, "Do I want my child to achieve academic success so he or she can go to college?" If yes, the other questions are: Are you preparing your child by your actions at home and as an involved parent so he can go to college? Are you preparing financially? Are you displaying and creating a college-going attitude and home environment? Do you know enough about getting your child to college? Do you know what you don't know? Are you seeking support? The steps and investments you are taking now in getting your child to college are signs of your level of commitment to your child's success.

    A parenting investment includes saving money if your child is going to college. If your child is unborn or born, how much money have you saved? Are you ready for college? That is a sign of your level of commitment to your child's success. Let me be clear about paying for college: while not all parents are not able to pay for college, that does not mean that your child should not be groomed and prepared for college as the next step. Don't limit your child by what you feel you are able to do or not do. If you know you will not be able to pay for college, your child deserves to know that; discuss it while encouraging them about other ways to pay for college. As a teen, I knew that I was paying for part of my college education; I knew I would take out loans. I am not opposed to taking out loans for college nor am I opposed to encouraging students to do the same. If I take out a $150,000 loan and I'm making about that each year, then who is winning? I'm winning – that is a worthwhile investment in me. That's a worthwhile investment in me making 50 times that amount over the course of my working career, a valuable investment indeed. Provide that clarity about paying for college with your child. Those are important conversations to have.

    What does your child want to do for a career? Do his gifts/talents even fit that career? The way your child plays, spends his time, and gets his attention – all reveal to you what interests him. And whatever his passion is, his vision is – it comes from him – it came from God - so that makes it very real and worth paying attention to for signs of direction. In order for your child to be most successful, feed that vision that is coming from him instead of focusing on what you wish for your child to become. You have your own opportunity to walk in your vision for yourself; allow your child his for himself. How much you invest in your child's passions and talents is a sign of your level of commitment to your child's success.

As a high school educator and principal for the last 18 years, enough cannot be said about the role of parent involvement in a child's life, as it is often the best predictor of academic success and educational achievement. A key area where parents and our society miss this mark is that we think parent involvement is only valuable up to a certain point, generally high school. Let me tell you: parent involvement is needed for all 13 years of school and then for at least the first year of college. You will not get this time back so you must be actively parenting and partnering now. You will not get a "do-over." What you sow into your child now is the seed that will produce a crop and grow into the harvest. How committed are you to a large and bountiful harvest?

At ASA Academy (the private school designed for African-American children grades 6 – 12 that I co-founded), I introduced a parent assessment tool called Principal Kafele's 50 'I's for Effective Parenting. This strong set of questions for African-American parents can also be used as affirmations to help focus your parenting and identify areas where you may have gaps you need to close, as well as acknowledge areas where you are excelling. At ASA, we even took it a step further and created the same list for students to assess what they felt they were learning from their parents as it related to the list. It was eye-opening to say the very least. I invite you to do the same with your child when you are ready for that type of delving into your educational parenting as it relates to your African-American child. Graciously, Principal Baruti Kafele gave me permission to use and publish the list for the *African Children's Manifesto*. I am deeply grateful to him, as his permission speaks to the unity, shared gifts, and teamwork that needs to be more intentional in our community for the betterment and success of our youth. The list is also published in his book, A Black Parent's Handbook to Educating Your Children (Outside of the Classroom), which I highly recommend.

Please write a "yes" OR "no" OR "maybe" next to each statement.

1. I am a parent to my children.
2. I am my children's first teacher.
3. I require my children to read books and newspapers daily.
4. I require my children to write early.
5. I read to my children.
6. I require that my children read African-centered literature towards their life-long study of their history.
7. I educate myself in order to educate my children about their history.
8. I teach my children about the struggle and their roles in the struggle.
9. I talk to my children about having pride in who and what they are.
10. I conduct myself as a role model for my children. I lead by example
11. I remind my children that they represent me at all times.
12. I spend quality time with my children.
13. I communicate with my children regularly – both speaking and listening.
14. I have high expectations for my children, despite my own setbacks.
15. I constantly encourage my children to search for the genius and creativity that lies within them.
16. I constantly challenge my children to achieve academic

excellence.
17. I hold my children accountable for achieving academic excellence.
18. I strive to motivate, educate, and empower my children daily.
19. I do not accept mediocrity from my children.
20. I tell and show my children that I love them.
21. I don't ridicule and demean my children.
22. I refrain from negativity in my interactions with my children.
23. I take my children to African-centered educational programs and activities.
24. I expose my children to a wide variety of activities.
25. I assist my children with their homework.
26. I review my children's homework.
27. I require that my children study – even when they do not have homework.
28. I attend functions and meetings at my children's school.
29. I go to my children's school to meet and interact with teachers and administrators.
30. I encourage my children to believe in themselves.
31. I assist my children with determining a purpose in life.
32. I assist my children with understanding that they have a historical obligation to achieve.
33. I encourage my children to be determined to desire success from within.
34. I encourage my children to develop a vision for success.
35. I require that my children are goal-oriented.
36. I talk to my children about societal issues and problems relating to individual and community empowerment.
37. I talk to my children about expected and acceptable behavior both in and out of school.
38. I discipline my children appropriately.
39. I teach my children positive values.
40. I teach my children about household responsibilities,
41. I teach my children conflict resolution.

42. I teach my children coping and survival skills.
43. I monitor my children's media exposure.
44. I monitor who my children spend their time with.
45. I provide for my children while not depriving them of their needs.
46. I teach my children about good hygiene and grooming.
47. I monitor my children's attire and overall appearance and have a say in what they wear and how they wear it.
48. I talk to my children about respecting adults.
49. I talk to my children about proper relations with the opposite gender.
50. I talk to my son about respecting, valuing, appreciating, and getting along with other Black men.

For some parents, the above statements are difficult and challenging on several levels. That's okay; you are taking the time to reflect, re-tool, re-educate, and empower yourself now. In order for your child to succeed in school and life, you must get in touch with your expectations and act/make choices accordingly. Again, you are not holding *African Children's Manifesto* without the intention of holding to the charge you have been given. Be gentle with yourself, commend your willingness and take action where you are clear and where your spirit is leading you.

"Vision is the Physician"

Every person holds a vision for how they choose to be in the world. I believe that your vision is communicated to you from God, and when we are tapped in to our spirit, we are able to see our vision and how to live and walk in that vision more freely. Your vision can be whatever you choose; some people have grandiose visions and some people have more simple visions. Both are absolutely fine because it's your choice. While your vision is your choice, the way you allow the vision to unfold through you is also your choice.

"Vision" sounds very fancy but it's really a mode of seeing or conceiving what is pictured in the mind or senses; the power of imagination to see what you want your reality to be. That's what a vision is. When you see your vision in your mind, then you have to step back and ask, "What are the steps and goals that I need to do to achieve that vision? Am I in alignment with my actions to even achieve that vision?" It's important that you have a vision for your role as a parent and for your family. Have you ever written a vision for your self? For your family? For your parenting? I encourage you to take the time to do so. If you don't know your vision, sit and have a good conversation with yourself and with God. Sit and get clear about your family lifestyle to achieve a college-going culture. Ask questions: What must I embrace to achieve the vision? What must I release? What gifts do I already bring? What kind of support do I need to bring the vision alive?

Your vision as it relates to parenting is about parenting with the end in mind. That means, parenting not only for college, but for those children that will not be going to college and parenting for beyond college- parenting for how your child takes what you instilled in him to live his life. Again, your child has a vision too. Your job as parent is to equip your child to live his vision, not create or choose his vision for him.

Concrete Strategies, Actions, Tasks, and Tools for Parent Champions™

After reflection and vision-building, it's time to take action where you are clear. And it's just that: while you may not be ready to do it all or not need to do it all, you are always at a place where you can make one type of change – large or small – that will create a new trajectory in a better direction that serves you and your family.

Your home is a place where you prepare your child for life and for where he spends most of his time: at school. Because of this, your home – whether it's a studio apartment or a mini-mansion - is a place where your child learns and validates your academic expectations for his success. I can not stress enough how your expectations of how you expect your child to perform at school must be created in your home first – through your vision, your narrative, and your actions. Remember, your vision sets the tone for your child's personal vision and your narrative must be louder than the other narratives your child is exposed to. You must limit his exposure to other visions and narratives. This is best done by one structured action: enforcing daily study time with limited television.

Limited Television

While teaching at ASA, we learned that a non-ASA family had a rule in their home: no television Monday – Thursday. Prior to creating this rule, this scholarly family was struggling with their very smart children to focus on school and produce quality work. They knew they had to do something impactful to show their children what they meant about the importance of school so they instituted this house rule – for everyone. This also meant that they had to up their parenting game (refer to "50 'I's for Effective Parenting" #10).

Our children have to understand that we are preparing them for their lives, not watching other's vision through the "tell-lie-vision." When the child knows there is no TV to watch, they stop rushing to get work half-done; they stop rushing to get less organized; they stop rushing to study less; they stop rushing through the reading assignment…all because they are not rushing to a scheduled TV show. They will see they are on YOUR schedule – the schedule of excelling in school and preparing for college. TV will become less important. The DVR is great if you have that and can record shows to watch later. Sometimes, you can even use TV as a reward.

When we instituted this request to ASA Families, many families said "Yes," and then reported an increase in peace in their homes, greater quality family time (they were not in different rooms watching different things), and, of course, we were all able to report an increase in the quality of academic work and attitude that was really the central goal of the implementation.

As you take control of the peace and schedule of your home, I cannot suggest strongly enough that you confiscate cell phones every night. Our children are not sleeping because they are using social media or texting or talking well into the early morning. They have told me this themselves and we see the evidence – fatigue, low achievement, and a bad attitude/mood due to fatigue. We must help children to help themselves, so please take those cell phones every weeknight. I think we can all agree that no one is calling your child in the middle of the night for an emergency that they truly have the capacity or resources to solve.

Meditation

From my own 20 years of daily conscious meditation time, I deem meditation as a critical requirement to do some of your best thinking. Plus, it's a wonderful way to bring peace to your home, spend free quality time with your child, and create higher levels of daily achievement for you and your child. There are divine ideas waiting to be given to you and your child, but we have to stop and tap in. Academic achievement, greatness, and genius also require a level of fostered creative intelligence. Creative intelligence requires quiet time to develop. This is often underestimated and not discussed in our society as a way to be smart. This creative intelligence is often referred to as meditation, which includes several philosophies about meditation and how to meditate. For my own daily practice and what I teach to others of all ages is to sit comfortably and quietly with your eyes closed and simply breathe. Allow your body and mind to become still as thoughts simply flow in and out. Anyone can do it. It's generally different each and every time, and the more we do it, the easier it becomes.

    At ASA, I taught students as young as sixth grade to sit for 20 minutes every morning without interruption. As a school of sixth to twelfth grade students and teachers (parents would stay and join us too), we would "sit" each morning to get focused and ready for our day of learning as a community. There were kids who would say, "That changed the way I lived day to day." You could see if they didn't meditate, their day was off-balance.

As a result of their positive experience with meditation at school, parents began to have their children meditate on weekends because it changed the energy and climate of their homes. And you can do it with your child – it's quality time. It's simply an act of creating peace and creating clarity. Further, meditation has been proven to reduce stress and anxiety. It's safe to say that the majority of our children – be it a by-product of school and/or home – are stressed or have some level of anxiety. It is challenging to focus on learning and school when stressed or anxious. It's important to note that even our students diagnosed with ADD/ADHD were able to sit and meditate and we all reported an increase in the positive behavior and focus during class as a result of meditation, not medication. Meditation is a tool for academic success that begins in the homes of Parent Champions™.

Be Proactive

One of the most important things that you can do as a Parent Champion™ is to be proactive versus reactive. In my career, I have so many parents that come to me when the child is already behind three or four years in reading.

From the very moment that you find out that there is a deficit in achievement or development or skill-building, you must take action. Taking action often means doing something extra, but most important, doing something that has not been done yet. If you do only more of what has already been done, then you may not get a better result. For instance, if your child is not doing well in math and you find this out six weeks into the school year, then that is the time that you increase study time AND get a tutor. Each year of school builds on the other. That's why children can fall behind and get "years behind" in learning; we let the problem go on too long believing (or hoping) that it will remedy itself, change later in the school year, or simply get better with a new teacher months later. This is all too often not the case. From personal experience on the student end of this, I have fond memories of being miserable with my college-student Algebra tutor after school. The reason I can look back "fondly" is because I know my mother acted like a Parent Champion™. She got me a tutor immediately when she saw that my struggle was more than what could be remedied by the teacher; it was obvious I needed more time and attention to gain those concepts. Some say tutors are too expensive, however I didn't keep my tutor for the whole year; my tutor was utilized only when I needed help filling in gaps in my understanding. We were not wealthy and my mother had to stretch her resources to make my tutoring strategic and pay off.

I also saw this same type of Parent Champion™ behavior by a 4.0 student at ASA. As talented and scholarly as this student was, she struggled to grow as a writer in my English class; she had the basics and general concepts down but her challenges came with extrapolation and voice. For some reason, I could not reach her in those areas of growth. Her mother got a writing tutor who focused in those areas for about two months. Taking initiative created change within weeks, and the improvement was obvious and worth the investment of time and money.

In addition, part of the beauty in that situation was that the mother (much like my own) did not criticize the teacher or complain that I was not reaching her daughter in this specific area; she acknowledged how much her child was learning yet also acknowledged that there are times when another teacher's voice is needed. There are times when we need to hear the same thing differently and because we learn differently, that is very valid. This is partially why extra help from the core teacher may not always yield results; there are times when you need a different style, different strategy, and different voice.

In summary, the key point is to take action where you are clear additional action is needed and do not waste time. Be proactive. A child who is behind only gets further behind unless other action is taken to make up for that time to get back on track.

Family School Partnership Act

Interestingly enough, our own state government acknowledges that we have to be proactive instead of reactive, hence California Labor Code 230.8, which is the Family School Partnership Act (Appendix). I continue to be astounded as to why this Act is not widely publicized and articulated in every school newsletter, website, and bulletin board. The Family School Partnership Act allows parents to take off from work for school-related business for their child (up to 40 hours per year). I have often written letters to the parents' employer citing this Act so that they may be more engaged; any good school would enthusiastically provide such a letter to you if necessary. Often, the first thing that comes to mind for using this 40 hours is to be at the school because you have been forced to, such as getting your child out of trouble. That would be under-utilizing this law, not an act of a Parent Champion™. This law serves you to serve your child by freeing you to partner with the school. Use this 40 hours to attend school events, volunteer, chaperone a trip, meet with teachers, or simply to visit the school at your convenience.

School Visits

This leads me to speak on the importance of certain considerations you should make before visiting your child's school. When you go to visit the school, it's critical that you stay at least half the day, especially at lunchtime. Because that's when what's really real is front and center – everyone's guard is down. What do you hear in the hallways? How are children engaging with each other? How is staff spending class time and out of class time? What is the staff morale/energy/attitude like? What is my child learning? What strategies is the teacher using? Simply lecture? Other activities? How does your child learn best – and are those techniques being utilized? Of course, go to your child's classes, but you also need to go to the classes of his next grade level because you want to make sure that the class is doing new things, not what your child is already doing. After all, remediation is not the responsibility of the school; the school should be teaching what the standards articulate and moving forward each month and each year. If the same school is doing another year of teaching and remediating at the next grade level, then the school is not even producing its own scholars at grade level, which is not a good sign.

"Effective School Partnering: Building the Bridge of the Home and School Connection"

A successful parent-educator relationship displays firsthand for the child that an entire team of adults is on his side and working to co-create his greatness and genius. When parents and educators work well together and share the common goal of fully developing a child, everyone benefits. This working relationship does not outgrow you or your child; it is expected to last until your child graduates from high school.

From the age a child enters school until he leaves school, his two most paramount and time-consuming "worlds" are those of home and school. As a child ages, he will spend more time in his academic world than he will in his home world. It is crucial that a positive relationship exists between the two worlds, as they should not operate in a void, one separate from the other. In my opinion, the spiritual principle "there is no separation" comes to mind as a concept for visualizing the home and school connection for the success of a youth. Further, parents and educators can provide each other with unique insights and different perspectives about the same child, culminating in a more complete understanding of that child's abilities, strengths, and challenges. The educator will know more about curriculum and the school culture, while parents will know more about the child's personality, tendencies, patterns, and family life. Further, as a child grows and matures, an educator can provide valuable insight into how the youth is developing a personal work ethic, work habits, and working relationships that may often look different than those displayed at home.

To launch the home and school connection in a positive way, the attitude a parent displays about school is crucial. This goes far beyond the "you need to do well in school" speech that parents often deliver. Because young children, in particular, identify strongly with their parents, the display of attitudes, values, and innermost feelings are contagious. They become embedded in the child's mind at the deepest levels.

In my experience as an educator, I have found many children's views about education, success in school, and respecting adults is often influenced by both the verbal and non-verbal expressions and feelings of the parent - YOU. If your experience with school was miserable, you might feel anxious about your child's school experiences. Your child will sense this, and it could impair her ability to throw herself wholeheartedly into learning. Further, for the child's sake, you need to put the past in the past and assume that your child's teachers, school, and overall experience will be positive and happy. Even if you didn't like school, the best way to help your child is to endorse his experience: Get involved, be positive, and trust his teachers. He will get the message: "School is important; I want you to engage fully."

After the right attitude and outlook has been set, it is important to address the "nuts and bolts" of the home and school connection. In addition to the full-time job that many parents have outside of the home, parents must look at educating their youth as their second full-time job. A parent does not have to take on the role of educator: however, it is crucial that the parent see his role as facilitating and overseeing the education of the child as a full-time job. Face it: it's a responsibility and a necessity. Many times, youth do not have the discipline, experience, or skill-sets to facilitate themselves in being successful in school without the guidance of a parent at home and a caring educator at school. Remember, "there is no separation."

Below are some tasks, action-items, and skill-sets to help ensure the home-school connection so that your children do well in school:

Have High Expectations: Let youth know that they don't have to be the best as long as they are doing their best! Set a high bar and put supports in place to reach that bar. Reward solid efforts as well as achievements. Look for growth, not perfection. Perfection only comes with the growth that practice brings (and practice takes time). Instill a sense of pride in your child's work. My mother would make me recopy my work until it was neat and then it got to the point where I would demand that of myself and take that level of care. Until we get to that point where we are demanding that level of care – having a high expectation for our children, the child doesn't really know to even do that. Often the expectations are not as high from teachers. The expectations of the classroom should not be higher than the expectations set at home for your own child. That level of pride, excellence, resilience, and quality will take your child far no matter whose classroom they are in or what college they attend.

Use Routines: As adults, we can govern and design our own routines. Work your child's routine into your own for the ease of time, learning, and spending time together. Make lunches together, get clothes ready for the next day together, read together, gather the next day's materials by the door together. By establishing routines together, a parent is also teaching his child or teen how to be organized and establish and follow his own routines that support successful habits of mind and action that, in turn, support school success.

Organization: Organization is a weak area for many children and parents, but it is a serious key to success. Routines, structure, and organization all work together to create a sense of peace and accomplishment. Organization sets the stage for success in the other areas of "doing school." Your organizational systems will look different based on your family dynamics, BUT no matter what your family dynamic is, I have two "best tips" that will improve your level of organization immediately:

TIP #1 – A Calendar – plot out <u>every</u> school date that relates to your child on your personal calendar AND post a large wall-calendar (showing all 12 months) in a central area of your home (back of a door, side of the refrigerator, hallway wall, etc.). You cannot be in two places at once. Having your child's school events on your work/personal calendar will ensure your availability to attend the school events. School events are priority over work and socializing. Remember, you cannot get that time back for your child's school, but your work will always be there.

TIP #2: Purchase a six-shelf sweater organizer and hang it in a convenient closet. Label each shelf with the day of the week and place your child's items for each day in the proper slot. For example, if you have soccer practice on Wednesday, then shin-guards, cleats, uniform, etc. would go in the Wednesday slot. This can be done each week as a family ritual on Sundays to prepare for the week, and maintained each night as you prepare for the next morning. I recommend that each child have their own organizer, and I recommend using it in the child's room or in a closet near the front door (or wherever you gather your items for each day). Your mornings will be much easier (and sane) with this system, and it creates autonomy for your child.

Meet and Greet: Plan a time to sit and discuss your child with her teachers. Discuss areas of success, improvement, and growth-goals. This is best done three or four times each year. A concerned, responsible educator would never avoid meeting or communicating with a parent. This is also a time to clearly express to teachers your expectations and plans for your child; let the teacher know what you are expecting of your child and how you can work together in holding your child accountable to ensure those expectations are met.

Express that you are there to create a win-win partnership for your child's success. Make it clear.

Support the School: Parents should attend school meetings, volunteer at least three times each school year, and participate fully in school (educational parenting). This shows youth that parents are connected to educators and the education process. This shows youth that everyone cares and "there is no separation." Again, be sure to start off the school year by getting a school calendar of dates, and then placing those dates on your own personal calendar. There is no need to accidentally schedule something or be caught off-guard with a school event that has been on your personal calendar since September.

READ!: Youth must read in every subject that they study. Please support good reading habits by going to the library, reading more for recreation, and always making sure that your youth is reading at least one book outside of his school assignments. Reading is like any other skill – you get better at it the more you do it. Further, parents can ask teachers for good general comprehension questions to ask about your child's reading. You can do this in the car or in line at the store: ask your child to tell you about the information he's reading. Dig deep by asking character names, details, setting, character relationships, etc. Make him think about what he is reading. This will improve verbal expression, articulation of ideas, and reading comprehension skills. It helps to train your child to look at reading to gain understanding. This also shows that you value his knowledge and opinion, building your own relationship and connection.

Monitor Schoolwork/Homework: Offer to help, but do not do the work. Look through the child's notebook/folder at least once each week to monitor progress, feedback, and assignments. You definitely want to use what we affectionately termed at ASA the "Let Me See It Policy." When your child tells you her homework is completed, you want to respond with, "Let me see it." This keeps your child accountable and you will be aware of the quality of work she is producing.

Be Connected: Having school-based conversations are part of an academic vision and preparing your child for academic success. Talking about the school day with young people shows that you care. Ask your child real questions about school. "How was school today?" can often be felt as generic. An authentically connected parent may want to be more specific such as, "Share two good things that happened during the day;" "Tell me about math class today;" "Who did you laugh with today?" "Who is the favorite character in the book you are reading?" Have fun thinking of one creative thing you can talk about with your child about school. If they cannot tell you good information above surface level answers, they are either not engaged or not learning. One or both of these things is at work and neither is good or even acceptable for your child's education.

Create a "Super Study Area": This is my favorite recommendation to parents who want to bridge the home and school connection. A "Super Study Area" will help a youth learn how to study and take homework time more seriously. This is something that really works, costs a little bit of money, and can ensure academic success for years to come. I would provide this information to parents upon enrolling their youth at ASA Academy. The concept is not my own and is taken from the book, *Full Esteem Ahead*. A "Super Study Area" can be made in a corner of any room in your living space (but avoid areas of distraction and family traffic). Here are the Steps to a "Super Study Area:"

Provide your youth with a good desk and comfortable chair. Second-hand shopping or asking for donated items works well for this.

Make sure there is plenty of light in the room. Besides ceiling light, consider additional light such as a desk lamp.

Use a file box or small two drawer cabinet to provide your youth with places to file letters, papers, projects, special documents, pictures, awards, etc.

Provide some shelves, stacking baskets, or crates for books and materials. Be sure there is a dictionary and thesaurus.

Stock the desk in an organized and useful way. Stock with supplies such as paper (lined & blank), pencils, pens, erasers, scissors, glue, tape, a calculator, and a hole-punch.

Provide a special calendar that notes homework, projects, and special events to be posted above the desk area.

If it's within your budget, provide a computer and printer in your home. I don't recommend having it at the youth's desk unless he is disciplined not to "surf/play" on the computer when he should be doing other assignments. Plus, a computer is best kept in a monitored area.

The "Super Study Area" really supports a youth's success because it conveys the importance of school and the structure to achieve from home. In addition, it is important to cement the homework routine effectively with set hours each night that will be spent in the "Super Study Area."

When a healthy relationship exists between home and school, parents and educators value the expertise that each of them brings to the compelling life-work of educating youth. When parents and educators work together to build the foundation of home and school as a team, everyone wins. Build the bridge of home and school with awareness, caring, discipline, structure, and love because "there is no separation."

"Take Action Where You Are Clear"

The bottom line is that we have to do more, and we have to do better. My father says "you've got to be ready so you don't have to get ready." Preparation is always more time consuming than the actual doing of what you have prepared for. Historically, we have had poor and impoverished situations and were able to achieve above-standard results. Today, we have an abundance of resources and above standard "everything" and we are yielding grossly sub-standard results. Achievement is not an issue of wealth; it's an issue of a parent's commitment to the success of their child. We cannot turn our children over to institutions to do the work that is our work to do. We have to do better. We must focus on educational parenting as much as parenting.

It is my hope that you have gleaned and identified a few next steps for yourself in regards to educational parenting and becoming a Parent Champion™. Your first step is simple: take action where you are clear. Your spirit will not mislead you; you know what you must first do.

We can win this race to close the achievement gap for our children. It will begin with one child at a time- your child first.

Call to Action

African-American students, like all students have the right to be educated by a group of concerned, invested educators who are culturally competent, culturally literate and culturally relevant. Who are more invested in the education of African-American youth than the very adults of that same community? We are the gatekeepers to their success. As concerned members of our community, we must ensure that every aspect of their education is accountable to the values that we hold critical. That means not only opening our own institutions, but contributing to those already in existence with both our time, ideas, energy, love and money. It means when our children attend schools not born in the African worldview, we ensure that those institutions uphold standards of conduct we deem culturally appropriate. We must reject curricula, policies and discipline models that isolate, marginalize and punish the African personality.

Teachers entering a classroom to teach should be equipped with a basic skill set. In addition to the obvious need for academic mastery of the subject matters, teachers must be masters of organization and masters of advanced lesson planning including back up lessons for different learning styles. They should build relevance, cultural competence/mastery and movement into the lessons. Mastery of classroom management is a must. Social skills such as displays of respect (including de-coding unspoken language, tone and embracing and becoming fluent in differing communication styles), in-class conflict management and relationship building with students should be prerequisites to teaching as well, with mastery being proven. Those who have no mastery of these basic skills should be required to complete supplemental training in these areas and then be required to prove mastery. This should be done universally as a component to teacher training, re-training and periodic assessments. All graduate credential programs must incorporate all of the above to ensure that teachers are entering the classrooms with the appropriate skill set.

Administrators (such as principals, directors, deans) entering a school system should also be equipped with a basic skill set. Discipline models (consequences for deviant behavior) that mimic prison or encourage students to enter the prison pipeline including detention, out of class referrals, suspension and expulsion should no longer be utilized. Models should be explored that not only embrace the European worldview and paradigm of control, but that also acknowledges and allows for the African worldview and paradigm of harmony.

Administrators should empower their teachers to create cultures of inclusivity in the classroom, break the "warden" pyramid structure and reward cooperative behaviors. Inclusivity, in contrast to exclusivity, would not remove students from the classroom setting or isolate or detain them after school. Teachers would be trained in "in-class" management, and identification of behaviors that although different, may not necessarily be disruptive if given a fertile educational environment. An example would be to *include* discourse in the lesson, instead of prohibiting it and offering negative consequences when it is demonstrated. Administrators would also have the task of ensuring all teachers have relevant training and periodically assess competency. Only when true multiculturalism is embraced, in both actions and thought, can our students begin to heal from the merciless onslaught of psychological violence that they have endured in education.

On a communal level, African-American community members must also increase our participation in the education of our youth. Textbooks with an alternative African worldview must be authored. Partnerships with existing independent African-American schools must be brokered. Further, we must embrace and nurture the maternalistic roots of our African heritage and stop criminalizing and making households run by women pathological. It has been theorized by some from within and outside the African-American community that households where a woman sits at the head are somehow lacking. This is a European view of family - that is, that nuclear families are the standard.

However, from Queen Mothers, to grandmothers to single mothers, the woman being head of household, community and even nations is not unusual in African families, organizations and societies. We must simply rescript what a healthy African-American family may look like. We must acknowledge that our children can be reared whole in non-nuclear families. Affirm that our community is not broken. We must parent all of the youth in the community and not just our own. We must offer knowledge, ideas and suggestions and breath new life into the on-going dialogue surrounding education within our community.

The educational system and its pending overhaul can take lessons from the healthcare industry. Fee for service models are ancient history and now healthcare providers, both physicians and hospitals are rewarded for quality and customer satisfaction. They are also penalized monetarily when those things are lacking. Health benchmarks are tracked and metrics of safety and quality are collected. Outcomes are both *objective* markers (similar to test scores in education) but also *subjective* indicators from the customers themselves (which, in education are the students and their families). This system of allowing the customer to participate in the evaluation of the system is painfully lacking in the educational system. We must inject ourselves in the conversation and effect curricula, school policy and teacher evaluations.

The call to us as parents is especially urgent. The work is hard, make no mistake about it. The stakes are high and cannot afford to be left to chance. As parents we are in constant evolution. As our children grow and learn, so do we. We are not only teachers, but doctors, counselors, and clergy to our children. We are their biggest advocates and must not be afraid to use our powers of persuasion and negotiation in their service. Let us join together in one voice, with one fist. Let us link arms in a show of strength and determination. Let us march onward into the horizon that is our children's future.

With the cooperation of parents, a "new and improved" educational machine and the wider community, we can begin to build a healthy, prosperous and whole African-American student.

African Children's Manifesto

Education is Universal. It is Empowering, Free and Boundless

We demand a culturally relevant, sensitive and respectful education.

We demand culturally competent, sensitive and respectful educators.

We demand educators with expertise and mastery of multi-cultural education.

We demand the assumption of our competence from our educators.

We will be nourished and nurtured by our educators.

We demand our "whole" being be educated by "whole" educators.

We hold our educators accountable to a high standard.

We will learn in environments free from cultural and psychological violence.

We will MOVE, laugh and relate to others.

We stand firm in our ability to thrive and teach others.

We reject mediocrity, false labels and low standards.

We embrace our intuitive mind as well as the academic.

We will have freedom of speech, movement and expression.

We will have freedom of spirit, thought and emotion.

We will multi-task and maintain positive relationships within the classroom.

We reject fragmentation, silence and control.

We embrace the social, living classroom.

We demand relevance and productivity in education.

We expect excellence from our education and promise excellence in return.

Introduction to Interviews with African American Males

Included on our website http://africanchildrensmanifesto.webs.com/ are short clips from interviews with African-American males - both students and a teacher. There are several themes that I found when questioning these men regarding the educational experience for young African-American males in our current system, and I will review a few of them here.

It quickly became evident that the *relationship* the African-American students have with the teacher and/or administration plays a critical part in how well they receive the education being provided. The presence or absence of trust between the African-American male student and educators was a persistent thread that ran through each person's recollection of their experiences. African-American males not only question the intentions of their educators, but also question the sincerity, integrity and competence of the persons charged with educating them. There is a clear preference for younger teachers - new graduates who are perceived to be more innovative, inclusive, energetic and tolerant and an aversion for more senior teachers who are perceived as apathetic and bland.

School (specifically high school) was described as lacking relevance to daily life, lacking flexibility for different learning styles, and lacking creativity. High school was compared to jail, but was also seen as the only vehicle to achieving college acceptance. Peer pressures were described as being both negative and positive at times, and all agreed that teachers should be evaluated not by a governmental standard, but by the students and their families regarding their effectiveness in teaching the subject matter.

Another theme that continuously reared its head was the issue of parental involvement. The men interviewed described that navigating the current educational system successfully required the active participation of family and friends on the student's behalf. The presence of an advocate for the student was necessary at all times to ensure the student's best interests were at the heart of all educational decisions made within the educational system. Parental involvement was also seen as a back-up resource for academic research, as mistrust of information given in class can be confirmed or disputed within the safety of the family home.

When interviewed regarding educational success, it was interesting that the men interviewed did not consider class size, availability of resources, governmental funding or socio-economics as primary determinants of African-American male educational achievement. On the contrary, the relationships they build with educators, peers and family and friends were viewed as critical in achieving and maintaining academic success.

VI. APPENDICES

Appendix 1

Family School Partnership Act Brochure: Questions and Answers

What is the Family-School Partnership Act?

The Family-School Partnership Act is a California law that allows parents, grandparents, and guardians to take time off from work to participate in their children's school or childcare activities. The law (Labor Code Section 230.8) first took effect in 1995. Its provisions were expanded in 1997 to add licensed child daycare facilities to the kindergarten-through-grade-twelve levels included in the original legislation.

What opportunities am I offered under this law?

If the following criteria are met, you may take off up to 40 hours each year (up to eight hours in any calendar month) to participate in activities at your child's school or day care facility: You are a parent, guardian, or grandparent who has custody of a child enrolled in a California public or private school, kindergarten through grade twelve, or licensed child day care facility. You work for a business that has 25 or more employees at the same location.

How should I account for my time off work?

The law allows you to use existing vacation time, personal leave, or compensatory time off to account for the time you use participating in your child's school or childcare activities. You may also use time off without pay if permitted by your employer. The employee, not the employer, chooses from the options that are available.

How can I take advantage of these opportunities?

Let your employer know in advance that you would like to take time off to participate in activities at your child's school or childcare facility. Although the law does not say how far in advance you should inform your employer, it is likely that rules are in place at your work site about reasonable notice for planned absences. And, if your employer requests, you are required to provide written proof of having participated at your child's school or child care facility.

If both parents of a child are employed by the same employer at the same work site, does the law allow them to take time off together for the same school or child care activity?

The parent who first gives notice to the employer has priority for the planned absence, although the other parent may also participate if the employer approves.

Does the law apply to parents who work the night shift or only to those who work the day shift? What about part-time employees?

All parents working full time, regardless of the shift they work, are allowed up to 40 hours per year. Because a night worker normally sleeps during the day when school is in session, that employee might ask for approval of an absence during the night shift in order to rest adequately for participating in activities at his or her child's school or child care facility. Part-time workers are allowed a proportionate number of hours. For example, half-time workers may take up to 20 hours a year. Teachers, even though they might work only ten months out of the year, are considered full-time employees and may take up to 40 hours per year.

What kinds of school or childcare activities may I participate in with my child?

Under the law, any activity that is sponsored, supervised, or approved by the school, school board, or childcare facility is acceptable. Examples might be volunteering in your child's classroom; participating in parent-teacher conferences, Back-to-School Night, Open House, field trips, or extracurricular sporting events sponsored by the school, school board, or child care facility; and assisting in community service learning activities.

I am a teacher. Is my employer required to pay for a substitute teacher during my absence?

Because teachers generally get neither vacation nor compensatory time off during the school year, their only options under this law are time off without pay and possibly personal leave, unless their collective bargaining agreement provides for other alternatives. The school district would cover the cost of a substitute teacher through the salary savings gained from the classroom teacher's time off without pay. Check with your personnel director.

Does my employer have the right to refuse my request for time off to participate in activities at my child's school or childcare facility?

If your employer has 25 or more employees at the same location, he or she cannot refuse the request. All such employers must comply with the law and allow you to take off up to 40 hours a year to participate in your child's school or child care activities. At least one of the options-using vacation, personal leave, compensatory time off, or time off without pay-must be provided to the employee.

My employer has an incentive bonus program for employees who take no unpaid leaves of absence. If I

take time off to participate in activities at my child's school or childcare facility, will my doing so count against me?

Yes, it probably will count against you. Labor Code Section 230.8 contains no clear answer to this question, but it seems reasonable that an employer would apply an incentive bonus program equally to all unpaid leaves of absence, regardless of the reason for the leave.

What should I do if I feel that my employer has discriminated against me for taking time off to participate in my child's school or childcare activities?

Your employer may not fire you, demote you, take away your benefits, deny you a promotion, or in any other way discriminate against you because you have chosen to participate in activities at your child's school or childcare facility. The law provides for civil penalties and compensation to the parents if such discrimination occurs. The law does not, however, give enforcement powers to a specific governmental agency. If you feel you have suffered discrimination, contact the Fair Employment and Housing Commission at 1-800-884-1684 or http://www.fehc.ca.gov or consult an attorney.

Title I Policy and Partnerships Office [Title I Policy and Partnerships Office]
California Department of Education [California Department of Education]
[1430 N Street, Suite 6208]
[Sacramento, CA 95814]
[(916) 319-0854]

Family School Partnership Act: Q and A
CDE, T07-077, English; Arial font
Page PAGE 1 of 3 California Department of Education 8/28/2007

Appendix 2

California Department of Education
California Code Excerpt
Labor Code Section 230.8 specific to Family-School Partnership Act.

CALIFORNIA CODES

LABOR CODE SECTION 230.8
(a)(1) No employer who employs 25 or more employees working at the same location shall discharge or in any way discriminate against an employee who is a parent, guardian, or grandparent having custody, of one or more children in kindergarten or grades 1 to 12, inclusive, or attending a licensed child day care facility, for taking off up to 40 hours each year, not exceeding eight hours in any calendar month of the year, to participate in activities of the school or licensed child day care facility of any of his or her children, if the employee, prior to taking the time off, gives reasonable notice to the employer of the planned absence of the employee.

(2) If both parents of a child are employed by the same employer at the same worksite, the entitlement under paragraph (1) of a planned absence as to that child applies, at any one time, only to the parent who first gives notice to the employer, such that the other parent may take a planned absence simultaneously as to that same child under the conditions described in paragraph (1) only if he or she obtains the employer's approval for the requested time off.

(b) (1) The employee shall utilize existing vacation, personal leave, or compensatory time off for purposes of the planned absence authorized by this section, unless otherwise provided by a collective bargaining agreement entered into before January 1, 1995, and in effect on that date. An employee also may utilize time off without pay for this purpose, to the extent made available by his or her employer. The entitlement of any employee under this section shall not be diminished by any collective bargaining agreement term or condition that is agreed to on or after January 1, 1995.

> (2) Notwithstanding paragraph (1), in the event that all permanent, full-time employees of an employer are accorded vacation during the same period of time in the calendar year, an employee of that employer may not utilize that accrued vacation benefit at any other time for purposes of the planned absence authorized by this section.

(c) The employee, if requested by the employer, shall provide documentation from the school or licensed child day care facility as proof that he or she participated in school or licensed child day care facility activities on a specific date and at a particular time. For purposes of this subdivision, "documentation" means whatever written verification of parental participation the school or licensed child day care facility deems appropriate and reasonable.

(d) Any employee who is discharged, threatened with discharge, demoted, suspended, or in any other manner discriminated against in terms and conditions of employment by his or her employer because the employee has taken time off to participate in school or licensed child day care facility activities as described in this section shall be entitled to reinstatement and reimbursement for lost wages and work benefits caused by the acts of the employer. Any employer who willfully refuses to rehire, promote, or otherwise restore an employee or former employee who has been determined to be eligible for rehiring or promotion by a grievance procedure, arbitration, or hearing authorized by law shall be subject to a civil penalty in an amount equal to three times the amount of the employee's lost wages and work benefits.

Official California Legislative Information (Outside Source)
Provided as a service of the California Dept. of Education
Title I Policy & Partnerships Office
916-319-0854
January 2004

parentalinvolvement@cde.ca.gov
l 916-319-0917

VII. FOOTNOTES AND REFERENCES

1 Campbell, V., & Bond, R. (1982). Evaluation of a character education curriculum. In D. McClelland (ed.), Education for values. New York: Irvington Publishers.

2 Huitt, W., & Hummel, J. (2006). An overview of the behavioral perspective. Educational Psychology Interactive. Valdosta, GA: Valdosta State University. Retrieved from http://www.edpsycinteractive.org/topics/behavior/behovr.html

3 Ani, M. Yurugu, An African-Centered Critique of European Cultural thought and Behavior

4,5 Townsend, B.L. Exceptional Children,"The Disproportionate Discipline of African-American Learners: Reducing School Suspensions and Expulsions."

6,7 Nelson, A.C. The Impact of Zero Tolerance School Discipline Policies: Issues of Exclusionary Discipline. NASP Communiqué, Vol. 37, #4. December 2008

Journal of Educational Sociology
"Formal Education and the Social Structure" W. Lloyd Warner
Vol. 9, No. 9, Attitudes and Education (May, 1936), pp. 524-531
(article consists of 8 pages):

National Middle School Association website
http://www.nmsa.org/

Psychiatric Bulletin
"Psychology of compulsory detention" Allan Beveridge
1998 Volume 22: 115-117

Understanding and Appreciating the Wonder Years
John H. Lounsbury

A Class of Our Own, Black Teachers in the Segragated South
Adam Fairclough

Acknowledgements

I would like to thank Tovi Scruggs and Ajuana Black for collaborating on this project. Many thanks to my sons Falating Nwagwu and Kitwana Nwagwu, as well as my dear friend Allen Scott Gordon for agreeing to be interviewed for the DVD and thank you to my nephew Yafeu Tyhimba for providing the instrumental music for the DVD. Thank you to my daughter Imani Pierce Nwagwu for assisting with production of the DVD. Thank you to Joy Coleman for the graphics in the book and Chamayne Pierce for allowing me to use the photo of her son (my cousin) Amari Brown on the cover of the book. Many thanks to Kelly Clark and JayVon Muhammad for contributing their experiences in interviews as well. I would like to thank Linda Johnson of Umoja House in Oakland, California and Mwalimu Evans of Mandela Children's Learning Village in Compton, California for teaching my children as well as countless others in the community. We ALL Thank you! I would also like to add a heartfelt thank you to my husband Akil El for being my co-pilot on the journey toward educating our children, for all of his support of my writing in general and his encouragement in the completion of this book in particular. Thank you to my parents Rendell H. Pierce Sr. and Lorraine Pierce-Gardner: My first and best teachers.